Praise for

One Holy Fire

"*One Holy Fire* will challenge you to cast off restraint and walk fully in the love of Christ and the power of the Holy Spirit. It's an awesome testimony to God's ability to change lives—even in the worst circumstances—if we will only trust him to use us, as Nicky has. What a great vision and calling this book presents to all of us!"

—BILL MCCARTNEY, founder and president of Promise Keepers

"Hundreds of people giving their lives to Christ in a single evening. Teenagers willingly devoting their time to feeding the homeless and sharing the gospel. Drug users miraculously freed from their addictions. Children born with physical deformities, now walking and leaping with joy. These are just a few of the miracles Nicky Cruz shares in *One Holy Fire,* a book that will open your eyes to the supernatural power of the Holy Spirit. You'll find your heart burning to experience the power of God's Spirit in your own life as you read how God is transforming those who have asked him to release his all-consuming passion in their lives."

—PAT ROBERTSON, chairman and CEO of the Christian Broadcasting Network and host of *The 700 Club*

"Someone has said that the two main purposes of the Christian life are to know Christ and to make him known. As you read *One Holy Fire,* you cannot help but feel these two great desires begin to burn in your heart. The hunger to know a holy God and to let his love, unconditional and pure, flow through you to others begins to stir deeply within. This is more than a book; it is a word to all of us."

—DR. RICHARD A. HEARD, senior pastor of Christian Tabernacle in Houston, Texas

"Nicky Cruz writes from the experience of life, and that makes this book so vital and relevant. As he shares his dreams and his heart, he points to the way the dreams have already become reality for him—and can for us too. This book is well written, engaging, and very challenging. Please don't read it if you're comfortable and want to stay as you are."

—DR. CLIVE CALVER, president of World Relief

"Nicky's life, as so candidly shared in *One Holy Fire,* inspires me to look beyond the facades of Christianity and seek intimacy with Christ. His example challenges me to live my life with the guiding question, *Does what I am about to do or say give God glory?* This book is a wonderful catalyst into deeper places of God's heart."

—DENNIS JERNIGAN, worship leader and songwriter

"I esteem Nicky Cruz as one of our generation's greatest evangelists. In his first book *Run Baby Run,* he ignited a passion for the lost, but in *One Holy Fire* he fans it into consuming flames. Nicky's experiences with the lost will give you both the desire and courage to share Jesus in your everyday life. You will not be the same after encountering his heart."

—JOHN BEVERE, author and speaker

"*One Holy Fire* is a must-read. Nicky Cruz is like no other, and what he has to say in this book will change every reader."

—REGGIE WHITE, former NFL superstar

"I agree with Nicky that the one holy fire of God will fill the coming generation of believers. Our youth are already taking a remarkable stand for God, and with teachers like Nicky paving the way, they are going to have an extraordinary impact during this century."

—TED HAGGARD, senior pastor of New Life Church
in Colorado Springs, Colorado

One
Holy
Fire

One Holy Fire

LET THE SPIRIT IGNITE YOUR SOUL

Nicky Cruz

WITH FRANK MARTIN

WATERBROOK
PRESS

One Holy Fire

Published by WaterBrook Press

2375 Telstar Drive, Suite 160

Colorado Springs, Colorado 80920

A division of Random House, Inc.

ISBN 1-57856-652-5

The Jim Cymbala quotation is from *Fresh Wind, Fresh Fire* by Jim Cymbala with Dean Merrill (Grand Rapids, Mich.: Zondervan, 1997), 27.

Library of Congress Cataloging-in-Publication Data

Cruz, Nicky.
   One holy fire : let the Spirit ignite your soul / Nicky Cruz, with Frank Martin.— 1st ed
      p. cm.
   ISBN 1-57856-652-5
   1. Cruz, Nicky. 2. Evangelists—United States—Biography. I. Martin, Frank, 1958– II. Title.
   BV3785.C87 A3 2003
   269'.2'092—dc21

                                                                        2002010801

Printed in the United States of America

To the many faithful partners of our ministry:
You are always there for me when I need prayer and covering,
with unwavering trust in me and in my mission.
I wish I could mention you all by name.

To my wonderful children,
Alicia, Laura, Nicole, and Elena.

To my precious grandchildren,
Nikolas, Isabella, Asher, and Mia.

And finally, to Gloria,
once again and always, from my heart to yours.

contents

foreword

Nicky Cruz is my friend. While he has blessed the Brooklyn Tabernacle—the church I pastor—many times through his ministry, Nicky has also inspired and enriched my own spiritual life.

I first met Nicky years ago at an evangelistic outreach we were sponsoring in downtown Brooklyn, not far from his old turf as a leader of the Mau Mau street gang. I knew about Nicky's dramatic conversion and how the Lord was using him around the world to reach countless thousands with the gospel of Jesus Christ. That night we witnessed the power of God's love as people of every color and background gave their lives to the Lord. We saw Nicky Cruz at his best—a true evangelist using his God-given ministry gift for Christ and his kingdom. That night also marked the start of a friendship I've grown to treasure deeply.

Nicky Cruz is a reminder that there is no limit to what the Holy Spirit can do. God has transformed Nicky from a fierce, hate-filled, violent person into a trophy of grace, someone whose example encourages every Christian to believe God for the impossible.

Nicky writes powerfully in *One Holy Fire* about the anointing and power of the Spirit because this has been the secret of his own dynamic ministry for Christ. Years ago when Nicky was making one of his regular visits to our church, a scene occurred that I will never forget. The auditorium was packed and overflowing with people. Suddenly an awesome sense of God's presence came as Nicky concluded his gospel message. As he spoke, a terrible scream arose from a young lady standing in the rear of the hall. "Help me Jesus," she cried as she staggered forward to the front of the church. "I can't take it any-more. Help me Jesus!" It was as though a bolt of spiritual lightning struck the audience. Nicky had not concluded his invitation to receive Christ, but soon people everywhere were walking forward under conviction of sin, drawn by God's amazing love for them no matter how they were living. It was a powerful demonstration of a Spirit-anointed messenger of God fulfilling his ministry for Jesus.

Nicky Cruz is absolutely on target as he writes of the critical moment of time we live in and the fantastic potential for Spirit-filled, Spirit-led believers to extend God's kingdom around the world. What does it matter what Satan is doing if the people of God are moving in the power of God's Spirit? If a former gang leader from Brooklyn can turn countless people to Christ around the world, what is holding us back from making a big difference for Jesus?

One Holy Fire can change your life and set you ablaze for God.

PASTOR JIM CYMBALA
THE BROOKLYN TABERNACLE

one holy fire

I tell you the truth, anyone who has faith in me will do what I have been doing. He will do even greater things than these, because I am going to the Father. And I will do whatever you ask in my name, so that the Son may bring glory to the Father. You may ask me for anything in my name, and I will do it....

And I will ask the Father, and he will give you another Counselor to be with you forever—the Spirit of truth.... You know him, for he lives with you and will be in you.

JOHN 14:12-14,16-17

A Gift to Embrace

God is the giver of amazing gifts, overwhelmingly wonderful gifts. But there's such a thing as our not knowing how to receive them. That was the case for me when my firstborn child, Alicia, arrived at Presbyterian Hospital in Brooklyn, New York.

I was only twenty-three at the time, a young married man with a horrible past and a relatively new faith in the Lord. I was still trying to figure out how to be a decent husband to my beautiful bride, Gloria, and suddenly I found myself faced with the task of being a father to a precious little girl, as well. How could I possibly measure up?

Just a few years earlier a court-appointed psychologist had told me that I would never be normal. Five times he looked me in the eyes, point blank, and said, "Nicky, there is no way you can ever have a normal family. With a past like yours you'll never be able to make a marriage last. You'll be a wife beater, and you'll abuse your kids if you ever have any." He also told me the reason: "You have a dark side in your life—a side that's killing you, slowly but surely. You don't know how to love, and you don't know how to be loved."

Now here I was, a new husband and father, and those words haunted me at every turn.

From the moment we brought Alicia home from the hospital, Gloria could tell something was wrong. Several times I caught her watching me from across the room as I would bend over our daughter's crib and make faces. I'd tickle her under her tiny arms and brush her face with my hands, but I never picked her up. I didn't know how.

One evening, when Alicia was four weeks old, Gloria decided to confront me about this. I had just taken a shower and was leaning over our baby's crib, making gestures with my mouth and laughing at her reactions. Gloria could no longer keep silent. "What's the matter, Nicky?" she said. "What are you afraid of? Why don't you ever hold our baby?"

I didn't know what to say. I was too proud to admit my fears, so I just stood looking at her, speechless.

There was a lot of my background that I'd kept hidden from Gloria. She knew that I had a sordid past—much more brutal than most—but I'd never told her just how painful and abusive my childhood had been. I was convinced that she never would have married me if she'd known about the horrible things I had experienced—and done. So I never told her everything.

"Tell me, Nicky," Gloria persisted. "Why don't you ever want to hold Alicia?"

Finally I said to her, "I don't know how."

She seemed surprised by my answer. "Then let me show you," she said.

Gently she scooped Alicia into her arms and instructed me to extend my hands toward her. She slowly placed Alicia into my arms and told me to bend my elbows and let her roll toward my chest. I did as she said, as slowly and gently as I knew how. I'd never held a baby, and I was afraid I might hurt her.

I wasn't wearing a shirt, and as I held her tiny body against my chest, I could feel the warmth of her soft skin against mine. Her eyes were open, and she was looking up at me, smiling, cooing. At that instant a wave of emotion began to well up within me. It wasn't what I expected. The feeling was like nothing I had ever experienced. As I held my precious daughter tightly against my chest, I could literally feel the tenderness and love running through my heart, right down to my soul. It was overwhelming. Tears began forming in my eyes. Such emotion. How could I have possibly prepared myself for such a moment of pure and innocent love?

For the first time in my life I understood what it meant to be a father—to be part of a family. It was as if God was telling me, *Nicky, this is my gift to you. You've trusted me with your soul, and now I entrust you with this beautiful child. Never forget that she belongs to me. Take care of her. Protect her. Teach her. Love her as I have loved you.*

In a million words I couldn't describe the feelings of awe and gratitude that came over me at that moment—the feelings that completely enveloped my heart and spirit as I stood cuddling this precious gift that God had so graciously given me. It was a gift that I didn't deserve and could never repay. I suddenly saw Alicia as so much more than a child; she was my future, my chance to start over, my chance to restore the years I had wasted.

My past was over. This was my life, my new destiny and responsibility before God.

I pledged to Jesus that from that moment on, I would faithfully care for my daughter—I would willingly do anything for her, even die for her. I suddenly understood as never before the importance of a child's coming into this world and how to receive such an incredible gift from God. I understood my responsibility as this child's father to be the strong and caring masculine image in her life, her hero. I would not shirk that responsibility, and I committed to God that this child, and any other child he chose to entrust to my care, would faithfully follow their Savior. No one was going to tear my children out of the loving hands of Jesus!

The battle for the souls of my children began at that very moment.

And also in that moment I finally understood what it means to receive an irrevocable, irreplaceable gift from the Savior.

If you are a believer in the Lord Jesus Christ, then you, too, have been given an incomparable gift by God—the gift of the Holy Spirit. God has entrusted to each one of his followers a measure of his power, a small piece of himself. It is a gift that none of us deserve, and one that we can never repay, yet he gives it freely and willingly to all who put their trust in him.

But with this gift comes great responsibility. Through the Spirit's power we are to take the message of God's love to the world around us—to use our position and authority in Christ to not only teach the world how to live, but to lead others into the arms of the Savior. It's an honor and a responsibility that should not be taken lightly.

MY MOST SIGNIFICANT MESSAGE

Thirty years ago my first book was published. *Run Baby Run* is the story of how God saved me from a life of hate and violence in the street gangs of New York, and the book continues to sell well, ministering consistently to the most helpless and hurting of our society. Prison chaplains around the world use it as a tool for outreach in their ministries, and it's even required reading in high schools all over the United Kingdom and Finland.

After *Run Baby Run* I wrote a number of other books attempting to expose the anger, violence, and hopelessness of life in the inner city. Each one offered concrete solutions to solving these problems, and the Lord has graciously blessed those efforts. We've been able to reach millions with our message of hope. Since my last book was released eight years ago, I've been approached by a number of publishers who wondered whether and when I was planning to write again. I never entertained those offers because I didn't really have anything new to say.

In the past several months, however, that has changed. God has planted in my heart a new message of hope as well as a deep burden to share it. This message is about freedom and spiritual abundance, about living a life in complete communion with Jesus, about breaking through our earthly limitations and making a powerful impact on the world around us. It's about you and me finally finding our places within God's magnificent kingdom on earth. It's about seeing people the way God sees them. Most of all, it's about learning once and for all to embrace the supernatural strength of the Holy Spirit and allowing him to release his wisdom and power within us. What a transformation we'll experience as we discover and embrace God's unmatchable, unmistakable power in our lives.

I believe this is the most important and significant book I've ever been called to write. That belief has nothing to do with the messenger and everything to do with the message.

WHAT I HAVE SEEN

Over the past few years God has given me a vision of the future. He has shown me a coming time when the Holy Spirit will move into the quietness of the night and stir up our children as never before. They'll be like the young boy Samuel in the Bible who ran to Eli because he didn't know whose voice was speaking to him in the darkness. I have seen how these children will run frightened into their parents' bedrooms at night, not yet realizing that it is God himself who is speaking to them.

God is calling our children to make a difference. He knows that so many of their parents have not fully surrendered their lives, their time, and their energy—their hands and feet and minds and hearts—to his control, so he's calling the children of our time to fill the gap.

My message to the parents of these precious children is this: Do not stop them. It is God himself calling them. It is his fire, his Holy Spirit, preparing the way for the greatest transformation ever to take place in the world.

So many young people are restless, tired of going to church where everything is the same routine. They want to see the Holy Spirit in action. They want to experience all of Jesus *now!*

I have seen a coming time in churches and in Christian colleges when these young people will stand up and speak out. They won't be doing so in rebellion but in sensitivity. They will demand that we put away our own wants and desires and let the Holy Spirit speak.

And I have seen that in every university in America—in this same spirit of sensitivity and sincere desire—they will stand and demand truth from their professors. They will insist that we restore and possess what has been so weakened and lost in this country—a respect for God, a love of country, and a deep devotion to parents and family.

I have seen a coming time when the Holy Spirit's force and pressure will bring about the changes God intends through our repentance and honesty and loving obedience. Our sin and doubt and faithlessness must be confronted and rebuked; the Holy Spirit will come to consume all those things, and he will be a healing force, the Spirit of wisdom and power and compassion.

I have seen how the Spirit's fire will move from coast to coast in this land, in the north as well as the south.

And already God's Holy Spirit has begun doing all these things.

A DYNAMIC FUTURE

The world today no longer accepts a belief system rooted in tradition and complacency, that is, "doing church" the way we've always done it. The next generation will either see the power of God working in their lives in real, tangible ways, or they'll have no use for our message and no interest in following our Savior. They need to see a consistency between our life and faith. If they don't, they'll reject us as well as our Lord.

The days of stale denominations filled with lukewarm believers are over. The ones that aren't already dead and buried soon will be. And I for one won't mourn their loss. I just feel sorry that they'll never experience the joy of reaching the world for Jesus and seeing what he could do through and in them as a church body if they would only open up and allow him.

But I'm not discouraged, because I've seen the future of the body of Christ, and it's an exciting one. God is doing a work today in the hearts of young people that's as real and dynamic as any revival in recorded history. Every day my ministry takes me into the lives of inner-city kids, the most unreachable souls in our society. These kids are as hard and angry and lost as any group on earth. Yet our message is getting through to them. The walls are coming down. They're coming to Christ in great numbers, and when they do, their newfound faith is real and genuine and life-changing.

Many of these kids become our most powerful and effective evangelists. They don't rest until every one of their friends and family joins them in their new walk with Christ. The Holy Spirit burns within them like a furnace, a raging holy fire in their souls, just waiting to explode upon the world. They call upon God to work miracles in and through them, often in ways that many of us would be afraid to ask or imagine, and he isn't letting them down. God is loosing his Spirit on these kids in magnificent ways. And they're turning their worlds upside down.

What would happen if every believer in this country caught that kind of passion and vision? What if each of us possessed the same burning desire to change the world as the inner-city kids I work with? What if we allowed God's Spirit to release his power in our lives as he has in theirs? Would the world ever be the same?

In the pages to come, we'll explore that glorious possibility together.

PART 1

The Fire

[Love] burns like blazing fire,

like a mighty flame.

Many waters cannot quench love;

rivers cannot wash it away.

SONG OF SONGS 8:6-7

The Light of Israel will become a fire,

their Holy One a flame.

ISAIAH 10:17

Hear the word of the LORD. This is what the Sovereign LORD says: I am about to set fire to you, and it will consume all your trees, both green and dry. The blazing flame will not be quenched.... Everyone will see that I the LORD have kindled it; it will not be quenched.

EZEKIEL 20:47-48

He will baptize you with the Holy Spirit and with fire.

LUKE 3:16

For this reason I remind you to fan into flame the gift of God.

2 TIMOTHY 1:6

For our "God is a consuming fire."

HEBREWS 12:29

CHAPTER ONE

A Face
I cannot Forget

She couldn't have been more than six or seven years old. Big brown eyes. Beautiful skin. Her dark hair was pulled back tightly in perfect cornrow braids on the top of her head, ending just above her shoulders. Brightly colored beads dangled at the end of each row. Her clothes were faded but neat and clean. And she had the face of an angel, innocent and pure.

I'm surprised I even noticed her, given the number of people scurrying about and the amount of activity surrounding the area, but I did. And I couldn't bear to look away.

It was late in the evening, in the heart of Houston, Texas, deep inside the inner city. Our ministry, TRUCE, was preparing for an evangelistic crusade at Reliant Arena, and we were in the streets inviting people to come. We do this through a series of small neighborhood music concerts, each held on a different street corner of the city, always in the poorest, most violent sections of town. We call these roving concert outreaches "hit-and-runs."

In every direction there were drug dealers, addicts, drunks, pimps, hookers, homeless people, angry teenagers, and here and there, children much younger. To one side I saw a small group of teens dancing erratically. They were drinking, laughing, and shouting vulgarities. On a brick wall behind them, the words "RIP Spyder" gleamed in bold, freshly painted red-and-black letters. From experience I knew that this bizarre little celebration was a mourning service for a fellow gangster, probably killed by a rival gang. Retaliation was no doubt being planned.

On one corner were several ladies of the evening with big hair, high-heels, and skirts so short they left little to the imagination. For a few minutes they refrained from peddling their wares to listen to our music.

Beneath a streetlight, a handful of young boys were strutting about, several of them shirtless and tattooed, with bandanas on their heads and baggy pants hanging low on their hips. Each one was trying to look meaner and tougher than the kid next to him. It's a game I understood well, because I used to play it myself.

Around the corner, a few blocks away, several police cruisers sat in the darkness of an alley, watching and waiting for any sign of trouble.

And there in the middle of it all stood this sweet, innocent child. The longer I looked into her beautiful eyes, the more my heart sank. *What's to become of this little girl?* I thought to myself. *What chance does she have? Is she destined to become a prostitute, an addict, a product of the streets? At what age will her innocence be stripped from her, if that hasn't already happened? What does the future hold for this poor, beautiful child of God?*

"DON'T DO THIS TO THEM"

As the music played loudly, I saw the little girl begin to dance. She twirled in tight circles with her arms stretched above her head, like a ballerina. Then she leaped high into the air, laughing and bouncing with joy.

I wondered if she had any idea how frightening and perilous her world was. Was she even aware of the filth and evil that lurked around every corner, just waiting for the chance to devour her heart and steal her soul? The mere thought of it chilled me to the core.

A wave of compassion and anger flowed into my heart and soul. I could no longer contain my emotions. I stepped forward to the microphone we'd set up. I took it in my hand, motioning for our crew to lower the volume of the music. Then I began to speak.

"Look around you," I said, talking to the parents in the crowd. "What has become of our streets? Look at what we've allowed to happen, what we're exposing our children to. Doesn't anyone care? Have we given up hope so easily? These children deserve better than this. They don't belong in this type of world. They're our future. They don't belong here."

I walked over to the little girl, took her by the hand, and led her back with me to the front of the crowd.

"Look at this precious child," I said. "She didn't ask to be brought into this neighborhood. Look at her face, her innocence. Look at all of the children here. How can we do this to them? Parents, I don't accept this, and you shouldn't either. Don't let your kids grow up in fear and violence and hopelessness. Don't do this to them. Don't do it to yourselves. There is a way out, and his name is Jesus."

As I continued to speak, to share my heart and my testimony, I sensed a wave of repentance sweeping through the audience. Once again, God was taking my words and doing a mighty work in lost and hurting souls. A handful of people began making their way toward me with tears flowing from their eyes. Then a few more followed. To one side I noticed several young men leaving their gang friends and walking in my direction, heads bowed toward the ground. People everywhere were weeping under the conviction of the Holy Spirit, and soon the sidewalk around me was flooded with remorseful souls seeking prayer and salvation.

When it was over, dozens of people had given their lives to Christ, including my new little friend with the cornrows in her hair. I bent down by her side and prayed with her, asking God to come into her heart and protect her always. Then I hugged her and kissed her on the cheek.

"Thank you for praying with me," she whispered into my ear.

"God will take care of you," I told her. "You have an angel by your side, watching over you. God will not let anything happen to you. Don't ever be afraid."

A smile broke out across her face as she threw her arms around my neck and began to squeeze. I didn't want her to let go. With all my being I wanted to do something more, to take her home with me and protect her, to take her away from the filth and debris and evil that ravaged her neighborhood and defined her world. But I couldn't.

As I drove away, I noticed her still standing on the curb, waving good-bye. All I could do was wave back. In my spirit I knew that God's presence had made a powerful impact on the people of this neighborhood, that the cause of Christ had won a commanding victory over evil. Still I found it hard to shake my sadness.

AGAIN, A WAVE GOOD-BYE

Late that evening as I lay in bed trying to sleep, the image of those large, gentle eyes continued to stir my soul. Over and over I saw her, this picture of purity and helplessness standing in the midst of hate and violence. "Dear God," I prayed, "give me your strength. Help me save the children from this hell that we've created on earth."

As I stared into the darkness, tears rolled down my cheeks and onto the pillow. I couldn't hold them back. "Please watch over her, God. Wrap your arms around her and keep her safe from harm."

My only comfort that night came from knowing that God truly cares, far more than I could imagine. As I wept, I knew in my heart that he was weeping with me.

Early the next morning I awoke and readied myself for an interview with one of the local news stations in Houston. I was still exhausted from the previous night and considered rescheduling for another time, but I decided to go forward with it. The opening evening of our evangelistic crusade was just days away, and I knew we needed to reach as many people as we could in the city.

When I met with the reporter, she'd already heard about our hit-and-run street outreach concerts and immediately began asking about them. I explained to her that it was the best approach we'd found for reaching people in the inner cities with the message of the gospel. I also told her about the previous night's concert and the number of people who had received Christ. I could tell she was intrigued.

"Let's do our interview on that same street corner," she suggested. It sounded like a great idea.

We caravanned to the neighborhood, and her cameraman set up his equipment on the same corner where I'd spoken the night before. We were walking along the sidewalk, discussing the details of the interview, when suddenly the little girl came running toward me, her colorful cornrows bouncing with each step.

"Hi, Mister Nicky!" she said, extending her arms wide. I bent down and caught her as she threw her hands around my neck.

"How's my little angel?" I asked.

"I feel wonderful," she told me excitedly. "I slept so well last night—better than I've ever slept."

"I know you did," I told her, "because I was praying for you."

"Really?" she said, her eyes wide as saucers.

"Really," I told her. "I asked God to watch over you. And he did!"

She smiled and hugged my neck even tighter. To one side I noticed a cameraman quickly hoisting the camera on his shoulder and adjusting the lens, hoping to get a good shot for the news story. Somehow it felt strange and inappropriate. I wanted to tell him to stop, to turn the camera off and give me a moment to visit, but I knew it wouldn't do any good. Instead I just focused on the little girl, on those big, beautiful eyes. I told her again how special she was to me and to God and how much I enjoyed meeting her.

"Always remember that Jesus loves you," I told her.

"I will," she promised. "And I'll pray every night."

She stayed and watched the interview, smiling every time I looked in her direction. Later we talked a while longer before I had to say good-bye. She hugged me again, and once more I drove away, glancing back to see her standing on the corner, waving good-bye—still oblivious to the danger and evil that permeated her world.

Though it's been several months since that encounter, I've yet to pass a day without thinking of my precious new friend and those big brown eyes. I often wonder how she is. I pray and trust that God is watching over her. And I thank him for using that experience to once again, with the Holy Spirit's fire, renew in my heart a sense of urgency and passion for the lost.

CAN WE REALLY MAKE A DIFFERENCE?

In the past few years God has been working in my heart and life in a way I never expected or imagined. He has continued to use experiences and people—people like my little friend in Houston—to enflame in my soul a passionate hunger for his power, a fresh sense of compassion, a renewed vision for the lost—not just the lost within the inner city but in our homes, our schools, our churches, and our middle-class and wealthy neighborhoods.

It's a burning passion that I want desperately to share with others.

Someone recently asked me, "Do you really think we can make a difference for Christ in the inner cities?"

Without hesitation I answered, "Yes, we can. Of course we can. And not just the inner cities, but in every neighborhood in every corner of the world!"

I know it can be done. With the power of Christ and the Holy Spirit on our side, we can turn the world on its ear within a few short years, and we can literally take the message of the gospel to every person on the globe. And we can send Satan right back to hell where he belongs.

In every place on earth, God's message of hope and forgiveness is complete and compelling enough to bring people to their knees before God. I see it happen every time I speak to a crowd, whether it's a group of one hundred or ten thousand. But that repentance will come only when we, as God's ambassadors, embrace the power of the Holy Spirit and accept the call to boldly and unashamedly take that message to the world.

GOD'S CHANGE IN MY PLANS

Just eight years ago, about the time my last book was released, I truly believed my days in ministry were coming to a close. I felt I had done all I could, that God was ready for me to step aside and leave the work of evangelism to younger and fresher believers. I was tired. And quite frankly, I was looking forward to quieter days and more time at home. I used to joke that heaven for an evangelist is a world without suitcases. I looked forward to the day when I would never again have to board an airplane.

But God stepped in and changed those plans. In his divine mercy, he began a process of rejuvenation and healing in my spirit. And he has since gone before me with more might and power than I'd ever experienced or imagined.

When I least expected it, God ignited within me a renewed purpose and vision for my life. Just when I was ready to step out of public ministry, he called me back into it. And he did it in a way that only God could.

It happened just over eight years ago, on a dusty road deep in the heart of Mexico.

Help from a stranger

Chaos and confusion were all around me, as pervasive as the dust and smoke that choked the night air. Moments earlier there had been a deadly collision on this street in Jerez Zacatecas, Mexico. Moving on foot through the traffic halted by the accident, I had hurried forward to the scene.

Bodies and blood littered the street. On one side of the road were the crushed remains of a Jeep that had been filled with people. Strewn nearby were dozens of torn and tattered Bibles and crusade leaflets, the same ones my ministry partners and I, just minutes earlier, had been handing out to the people who responded at the end of our evangelistic meeting at a nearby stadium. In a ditch farther ahead was a car mangled beyond recognition.

I saw a handful of people hovering over the bodies of two women, perhaps a mother and her daughter. The bodies showed not even the faintest signs of life. I saw another woman lying in the dirt, writhing in pain and crying for help. Two people held a towel tightly on her leg. I could see the shattered bones of her knee protruding through the skin just below the thigh. "Hold on," they told her. "Help will be here soon."

As I walked closer, I was startled by a voice beside me, from within the crushed Jeep. "Nicky! Nicky Cruz! Hallelujah! Nicky!"

A VOICE GROWING WEAKER

I bent down as far as I could beside the Jeep's passenger window and peered inside, trying desperately to see the source of the cries. On the seat I could see a copy of my book *Run Baby Run,* the cover smeared with fresh blood and dirt.

"Nicky!" the voice continued. "Praise God, Nicky!"

As my eyes adjusted to the darkness, I could see the figure of a man pinched beneath the weight of the overhead cab, his legs crushed behind the steering wheel. His eyes met mine, and his arm stretched out in my direction. "Nicky," he said, his voice growing fainter. "It's so good to meet you, Nicky. What an honor."

"Sit still, friend," I told him. "I'll get you out."

The front windshield had been shattered by the wreck, so I ran around to the front of the truck and tried climbing onto the hood to reach the man through the splintered glass. But the metal gave way beneath my weight. Standing on the bumper, I stretched my arms out in the man's direction.

"Nicky Cruz," he said again, his arm still extended toward me.

"Hold on, friend," I told him. "Hold on." The broken glass hanging from the windshield sliced into my wrist, sending blood down the side of my arm. But I couldn't get close enough to help him.

The man smiled faintly, still gazing into my eyes. "Nicky Cruz. What an honor to meet you. Hallelujah! It's Nicky!" His voice was growing weaker with each word.

"It's good to meet you, too, my friend," I told him. "But please, save your breath. Help will be here soon."

Two of my ministry coworkers, Sonny and Julie Arguinzoni, had followed me to the scene, and I called out to them to help. Sonny and I crawled through the wreckage to the Jeep's driver-side door. Twisted metal mangled the frame, jamming it shut. Sonny and I pulled with all our might, fighting to work the door free, but it wouldn't budge. All the while the man continued to call out my name. "Nicky Cruz. Thank you for helping me, Nicky."

Stretching to reach inside the shattered windshield, Sonny and I tried in vain to pry some of the metal away from the man's crushed legs. Again our efforts failed.

"WHY, GOD, WHY?"

For several minutes we talked with the man and prayed that God would somehow spare his life. We laid hands on him and pleaded with the Lord to renew his strength, to keep him alive. Still, I could see in his eyes that he was slipping away quickly.

In the distance we heard the faint sounds of an ambulance. I prayed it would reach us in time, but the sound of the siren didn't seem to draw any nearer; the road must have been blocked by the stalled traffic—most of it consisting of people on their way home from our crusade.

"Help me, Nicky," the man said once more.

A burden of guilt ripped deep into my soul. *This is my fault,* I told myself. *If it weren't for me, none of this would have happened.* These people had come to hear me speak, to listen to my testimony, and now they were lying on the side of the road, either dead or fighting for their lives. It wasn't fair. And it wasn't their fault.

"Dear God," I cried, "Why did this happen?"

I looked back at the man in the truck. Suddenly his hands went limp and his head fell backward against the metal truck frame. His eyes stayed open. He was gone.

I climbed down from the wreckage and made my way to a corner of the back bumper. There I sat and cried, my face buried inside my hands that were bloody from the cut on my wrist. "Why did this have to happen?" I cried.

"Why, Lord? This is all my fault. If it weren't for me, these people would still be alive. Why, God? Why?"

A MIGHTY WORK

As I sat weeping, helpless and frustrated, my mind wandered back to the events leading up to this terrible tragedy. I couldn't understand why God would allow Satan to take such a wonderful and inspiring evening and turn it into a senseless bloodbath.

I remembered my trip with Sonny and Julie from the hotel to the stadium just a few hours earlier. I couldn't remember the last time I'd seen Sonny so excited. He and Julie, my good friends of many years and the founders of Victory Outreach ministries, had spent months planning and preparing for this crusade, and workers had been scouring the city to invite people to come. "We're expecting a huge crowd tonight," he told me. The stadium was not a large one, and Sonny wasn't sure how they would fit everyone in. "I just know God is going to do a mighty work tonight," he said. "I can feel it!"

We arrived at the three-thousand-seat stadium to find it filled well beyond capacity. Chairs had been brought in and set up, and still people were sitting on the floor around the stage and standing along every wall.

As I began to speak and share my testimony, I sensed something powerful in the air. Though I was physically exhausted from my grueling schedule, I suddenly found myself filled with energy. Rarely have I felt the Spirit of the Lord come upon me so mightily. I forgot about myself and was focused only on the lost souls there, on the pain and despair and confusion of those in the audience who didn't know Christ. And I prayed that God would bring me the right words to reach them and bring healing to their hearts and souls.

I told them of my days as a child in Puerto Rico, growing up with a warlock for a father and a spiritualist for a mother. I shared the stories of physical and emotional abuse and of the day, at the age of fifteen, when I was put on a plane to New York with nothing but the clothes on my back and ten dollars in my pocket. I described the fear and hunger that led me to steal for food in the streets and recounted the hate that quickly drove me into the arms of a dangerous street gang called the Mau Maus. I talked of the bitterness in my heart and the rage that took me to the top of their ranks, eventually making me their warlord and leader. I talked of the violence I had seen and the pain I had inflicted upon others, always without feeling or remorse.

Then I told of David Wilkerson, the skinny, out-of-place street preacher who dared to come onto my turf in New York to convince me that Jesus loved me. Though I cursed and threatened him, violently pushing him away, he never stopped sharing the gospel, never stopped loving me, never stopped telling me that Jesus died for my sins and wanted to love me if only I would put away my hate and let him.

As I stood in the center of the stage, sharing about the day that I finally gave in and fell to my knees before David Wilkerson and my gang—surrendering my life to God, begging him to forgive me of the horrible things I had done, the things that haunted me daily—I could feel every eye in the stadium focus directly on me. Sweating profusely in the sweltering heat, I pleaded for every soul in the stadium to do as I had done years ago. "In the name of God, don't leave here tonight without knowing his touch, without feeling his love in your heart, without giving yourself over to the God who created the universe, the One who controls everything.

"It takes a lot of guts to come forward in front of all your friends; don't think I don't know that. It took all the guts I could muster to surrender my life to God in front of my gang and the other rival gangs in our neighborhood, but I did it, and God has never stopped blessing me, never stopped loving me. Jesus loves you, and he wants you to give yourself over to that love. Please come, right now, and let me pray for you. Please! Let God love you and heal your broken hearts!"

As I pleaded on God's behalf, I could hear the sounds of weeping from every corner of the arena. Hundreds began to flood the aisles and make their way forward. Toward the front of the stadium, crusade workers had to remove chairs and bleachers to make enough room for the people gathering there. God was working mightily to bring people to conviction, and I could feel the exhilarating power of his Spirit loosed around us.

A Collision Meant for Me

There's no greater experience on earth than that of helping people come to repentance before God, of seeing lost and hurting souls finally lay aside their pride and their human efforts to save themselves, giving themselves over to the Lord's grace and mercy. To stand with those who just hours earlier had been steeped in sin and to witness the tears running down their faces as they beg God for forgiveness—it's the greatest joy life offers this side of heaven. And the joy is the same, whether it's one person doing this or one hundred.

After praying with this gathered crowd that night, I encouraged fellow Christians in the audience to find one or two of these new brothers and sisters in Christ and continue ministering to them. More than six hundred people were saved that evening, so we stayed for several hours, making sure that each and every one had been ministered to and received a Bible and that each person had left a name and phone number so we could contact them later. (I'm convinced that the follow-up campaign after our crusades—usually conducted by area churches supporting our ministry—is the most crucial part of our outreach efforts. Sadly, it continues to be the hardest part of what we do. Even so, each time we come to a city, the Spirit adds new souls to the weekly attendance of the churches that help us.)

When Sonny and I were sure that everyone had been taken care of, we made our way toward the back parking lot. He reminded me of a meeting I had later that night, so we hurried to our car and drove away, hoping to find a way around the congested traffic.

As we turned onto the main road, I noticed a Jeep full of people pulling up behind us, several of whom I recognized from the crowd that had walked forward to the front of the stadium. Some of them were hanging out the back of the vehicle, singing hymns and praising God. "That doesn't seem very safe," I said to Sonny. "I'm glad they're excited, but they really should be more careful." It was late, the streets and roads were dark, and I knew from experience that drivers in Mexico weren't always the safest.

Just then I realized I didn't have my Bible with me. "Sonny," I said, "I think I must have left my Bible at the stadium. I remember laying it on the podium." We considered leaving it, maybe having it sent to me later, but we decided it wouldn't take long to retrieve it. Sonny made a quick U-turn and headed back to the arena. He found the Bible on the podium, right where I remembered leaving it, and soon we were back on the road.

It was only moments later when we came across the accident scene. It was the same Jeep we had noticed earlier, and we were told that it had collided head-on with a vehicle traveling far beyond the speed limit and without headlights. Someone said the other driver was drunk.

A thought popped into my mind that sent chills down my spine. *This was meant for me. I was the one who should have died in this accident. These people are dead and hurt because of me!*

I'm the one Satan was after!

Sonny and I stayed with the people until an ambulance and the police finally arrived and began clearing up the wreckage. We made our way back to our car. Dirt and dried blood stained our clothing.

The shock of the event left us speechless and empty as we continued driving. No one knew what to say. The question stayed in my mind: *How could God have let this happen?*

TIME TO QUIT

That night I went to bed and tossed and turned for hours. I couldn't get the images and sounds out of my mind—the dead bodies lying on the road, the cries of pain, and especially the pleas of the driver crushed behind the wheel. All night I stared into that man's eyes, reliving my frantic attempts to try to reach him. Over and over in my mind I watched him die as I stood by help-lessly but praying that he would live.

At six in the morning I got up and slipped on my running clothes. I made my way down the hotel's back stairway and began running down the street, slowly at first. All the while, I couldn't shake the horrible images from the night before. I pushed myself forward, running harder, faster, trying desper-ately to dispel the memories.

I turned down streets I didn't recognize and lost track of the time. I knew I was close to the city's edge and wasn't sure I could find my way home. Even-tually I turned down a dirt road. My legs were beginning to quiver and my feet ached. Sweat ran down my face and back. Still I ran.

It should have been me, God! I cried out in my mind. *Why couldn't it have been me? These people didn't deserve to die!* I knew in my heart that if it weren't for my crusade, these people at this moment would probably be lying in their beds next to their loved ones, awaking to face another day.

I tried to convince myself that it wasn't my fault, that God had a purpose in letting this happen. *I should be grateful God protected me and has allowed me to continue in my ministry. I should be glad I'm alive. And at least the people who died were saved. That should make me feel better, shouldn't it?*

But the harder I tried to make sense of it all, the more confused I became.

As I wrestled with God, I began to wonder if perhaps he wasn't sending me a message. Maybe God wanted me to quit. Maybe it was time to step aside and let someone younger take my place. Maybe God was unhappy with the way I was running my ministry and had other plans in mind for my future. Maybe I was beginning to rely more on myself than on his power and guidance.

It wasn't the first time such thoughts had crossed my mind. I'd had a lot of frustration over the past months. My schedule had been wearing me down, physically and spiritually, for some time, and I'd been wondering when God was going to move me toward a simpler, quieter life. I'd been fighting Satan and his demons for more than thirty years. Hadn't I done enough already? I'd taken my testimony to more than thirty million people, and each time I told my life's story I was forced again to relive the hate and violence of my previous life. When was God going to let me move beyond this and rest, to spend more time at home with my family, to finally break free from the lonely life of a traveling evangelist?

The farther I ran on the dirt road, the more convinced I became. "Maybe this needs to be my last public crusade," I said aloud to no one but myself. "Maybe it's time to quit." I was surprised at the resolve in my voice. The statement sounded more like a decision than an inquiry.

I was still running, but my pace had steadied. My steps seemed sure and deliberate. *It's time to quit,* I concluded. *It's time to move aside and let someone else take the reins.*

A STRANGER'S COMMAND

I wasn't sure how to break this news to my wife, Gloria, and my family, or how they would accept it. Neither was I sure where my change in plans would take me. But I was certain of one thing: I had just completed my last public crusade. In my mind, the decision had been made.

As I continued to jog down the dusty road, it suddenly dawned on me that I was far from the hotel and from the city. The sun beat down as I surveyed the land around me. I was in the middle of nowhere.

In the distance I could hear the faint sound of a car engine coming toward me from behind. I turned to see a cloud of dust moving in my direction. I wondered if I shouldn't try to flag down the driver and seek directions for the shortest way back to the hotel, but before I could make a decision, the car blew past me, spitting a cloud of dust through the air. It was an old, tan pickup.

I covered my nose and eyes, waiting for the dust to settle. *Maybe another car will come by,* I thought to myself. *Until then, I'll just keep going and see what I find.*

Some distance in front of me, however, the pickup had stopped and turned around. Once again it was heading in my direction. *This is great,* I thought. *He's probably coming back to rob me.* Such things weren't uncommon on the back roads of Mexico. I hoped I was wrong but prepared for the worst.

The truck slowed and pulled close with its passenger door next to me. The windows were rolled down. Through the dust, I could barely make out the figure of a man sitting behind the wheel. He reached over, opened the passenger door, and called out to me.

"Nicky Cruz! Get in!"

His words took me off guard. How did he know my name?

Again he called to me. "Nicky, you're lost. Get in!"

"I don't feel well," I told him, somewhat surprised at my response.

He persisted. "Get in, Nicky. You need help."

I have a lot of faults, but naiveté has never been one of them. When you've spent as much time on the streets as I have, caution becomes second nature.

"You're nuts," I told him. "I'm not getting in your truck."

"Get in this pickup, Nicky," he said, this time with authority. "You're lost, and we're here to help you."

I peered through the dust to see if he had someone with him. He was alone.

"You need to get into this truck, Nicky. You can trust me. We're here to help."

To this day I'm not sure why I obeyed this stranger's words. He could have been sent to kill me or kidnap me. He could have been there to rob me and leave me for dead. I had no way of knowing. Still something told me to trust him, to get into the truck.

So I did.

CHASTENED

As we drove along, I noticed that the driver wore khaki pants and a white shirt buttoned all the way to the neck. His face was clean-shaven. The inside of the truck was dusty but orderly.

"Don't be afraid," he told me. "What happened last night is not your fault." His words took me aback, but I continued to listen. "Things happen in this life. We don't always understand, but we have to trust that God is in control, in spite of how it may seem. God knows you're hurting and confused. He knows you're tired and ready to quit. But I'm here to tell you he isn't through with you yet. You're not finished."

I sat quietly as he spoke. His voice was kind but convicting, his words bold and sure. He began detailing the events of the night before. He described the accident scene, both before and after I'd arrived. "I know you think it was your fault," he said, "and that you think it should have been you instead. But God protected you for a reason, Nicky. He's always watched over you, and he still does."

Then his voice took on a different tone. This stranger began to chasten me.

"It's not your place to question God," he said. "You don't have the authority to second-guess my Creator. He knows what he's doing even when you don't."

He placed his large hand on my shoulder. "I'd like to pray for you, Nicky," he said.

I bowed my head.

His words of prayer were real and authentic. He talked to the Lord softly and gently, with a deep sense of love and reverence. He spoke as a dear friend of the Creator. It was the most powerful and anointed prayer I'd ever heard. Tears of relief began flowing down my face as he continued praying.

Suddenly I knew I was in the presence of something holy. I wondered why I didn't recognize it earlier. I'd felt the presence of holiness before—many times in fact—but this was different. This time the feeling was more powerful and surreal. And this miracle from God was wrapped in skin and bones.

Before I knew it, we were pulling up to the entrance to my hotel. It didn't occur to me at the time that he'd never asked where I was staying.

"Thank you for bringing me home," I said through my tears. "Thank you for being here for me."

"I'm always here for you, Nicky," he answered. "But don't ever forget what I told you. God has anointed you with a purpose, and he will be the one to decide when he is through using you. It's your job to simply obey and continue the work you've been called to do. Don't ever forget that, Nicky."

As I walked from the truck toward the lobby entrance, still somewhat dazed, I suddenly wanted to see him one more time. *Maybe I should give him a copy of my book,* I thought. *And I wonder what his name is?*

I turned and ran back toward the sidewalk, but the truck was gone. I dashed toward the curb and fixed my gaze down the street, peering as far as I could in both directions. It had only been a few seconds, and he couldn't have gone far. Still, no truck was in sight. He had disappeared.

I made my way through the lobby and up the elevator to my room. I stood beside my bed, still shaking, my dust-covered clothes drenched in sweat. I dropped to my knees and began to pray.

"Thank you, Lord Jesus. Thank you for sending your angel." My eyes rose and fixed on the bright blue sky outside the hotel window.

"Jesus, I've sinned against you. I know I've disappointed you. Please forgive me for wanting to quit—forgive me for doubting you."

I crouched to the floor and buried my head in my hands. Tears ran through my fingers. I was so thankful to Jesus for this blessed gift he had given me. I couldn't believe this beautiful act of love my Father had shown to me, and my heart cried out in praise.

"Sweet Jesus, I don't know what you have planned for my future, but whatever it is, I'm ready. I've always been ready. And you've always been there for me. Use me, Lord. Show me what you want me to do next."

CHAPTER THREE

The Joy
of New Passion

As I've thought back on my angelic encounter on that dusty Mexican road, I'm convinced this wasn't the only time I've been visited by one of God's messengers. Most of us have had those visits at one time or another, though usually we were unaware. But I'd never had an encounter of such boldness and clarity, leaving no doubt about the identity of the visitor as well as the purpose behind the visit. This gentle servant understood his standing before God as well as his purpose. He'd been sent with a message, and he remained true to his mission. (When God sends an angel to speak to us, it's essential that we focus on the message, not the messenger.)

For several weeks after that experience, I felt a sense of peace and tenderness envelop my heart and spirit. When I told Gloria every detail I could remember about the encounter, she wept with joy. "God knew you were hurting, Nicky," she told me. "He wanted you to know how much he loves and cares for you."

"God is so good, isn't he?" I told her. We cried and prayed together, thanking Jesus for his kindness.

I also told my friend Sonny about it, and his response was just as tender.

But beyond that, I kept the story to myself. It was one of those precious gifts I wanted to keep mostly for myself—a sweet secret between my Savior and me. My prayers took on a sense of gentleness and warmth as never before. And my passion for God's purpose and will burned hotter than ever.

"Dear God," I prayed, "show me what you want from me. Give me your direction."

And I waited patiently for an answer.

A REFRESHING CHANGE

This new sense of fervency and zeal was a refreshing change for me. Though I'd always loved God and rejoiced in his calling on my life, I'd found myself growing increasingly weary and discouraged. Not with the work of evangelism—that part of my life has always been my passion and my lifeblood—but more with the daily frustrations of ministry and travel and organization.

Anyone who travels can testify to the sense of despair and regret you begin to feel when you spend so much time away from loved ones. Even when good friends travel with you, they're no substitute for your family, your precious wife and kids.

I couldn't begin to count the number of evenings I sat alone in a hotel room, nibbling on a sandwich from room service, staring out the window at billboards and streetlights, wondering what my family was doing. I'd try to imagine what Gloria had prepared for supper and what stories my kids had brought home from school that day. Often I'd pick up the phone and call, talking to them one at a time, trying to feel a part of things. And for a moment I was. Then I'd say good night and hang up and once again stare out the window.

How I longed to tuck my kids into bed and read to them, to kiss them on the cheeks and run my fingers through their beautiful hair, to lie in bed beside Gloria and talk of our day. At times the loneliness seemed more painful than I could bear. But morning would come, and the work of the Lord would once again keep my hands busy and my mind occupied—until the sun went down and the feelings of isolation would resurface once more.

What made these times even more distressing was the knowledge that Gloria and the children missed me as much as I missed them. At home it broke my heart every time I had to tell my kids that I was going away again. "Just for a few days," I'd tell them. "And when I get back we'll do something special." It was small consolation. I could see the disappointment in their eyes.

Also, as you might expect, loneliness often brings temptation. And the lonelier you get, the harder Satan tries to lure you away. Like any man, I've struggled with temptations of pride, fame, lust, and money. Years ago God put it on my heart to surround myself with a group of trustworthy friends and family who would keep me accountable. I trust these people to be completely honest and forthcoming if they see me getting out of line in any area, and they haven't let me down. It isn't always easy to receive correction or constructive criticism, but I've always pledged to listen without getting defensive.

I thank God for giving me Gloria, a woman whose heart hurts for the lost even more than mine does. I can't think of another woman on earth who has supported her husband the way she has supported me. Still, I'm not sure either one of us understood how much God's calling on my life would keep us apart. That time in my life was a true test of our relationship.

I've also been keenly aware of the risk Gloria took, because of my past, when she agreed to marry me. I brought a lot of baggage and destructive behaviors to our relationship, and I spent years worrying about whether I would be able to overcome my past and become the kind of faithful husband and father God wanted me to be—and the kind my family needed. I knew that on my own I would never be able to do that. But Jesus not only saved my soul, he also broke the curses of my past that plagued me—the curses of witchcraft, abuse, anger, violence, and sexual immorality. In spite of the many temptations to fall to sin, God's hand has always been with me.

Still, the loneliness and temptation of the road were very real and growing increasingly difficult to deal with. At times they would strip the joy completely out of my evangelism efforts.

THE GOSPEL AND PERSONAL GAIN

But long hours and loneliness weren't my greatest causes of frustration during those years. It saddens me to say that most of the stress I felt came from what I saw inside the body of Christ—in particular, among church leaders and pastors, Christian celebrities, religious entertainers, and high-profile evangelists. I'd seen many disturbing trends developing within the Christian movement, and it began to wear at me daily.

Anytime money is introduced into the mix with evangelism and Christian service, you expect to see priorities getting a bit skewed. Too often I saw greed become the primary force behind the ministries of many of my colleagues.

One particularly sobering example comes to mind. I was once asked to be the keynote speaker at a large Christian festival. It was being promoted as one of the largest religious gatherings ever assembled, sure to begin a new revival among young people. A large and impressive lineup of Christian celebrities and entertainers had signed on. Advance ticket sales started rolling in, and it soon became apparent that around twenty thousand people would be attending.

Long before the event there was a lot of discussion about the victory for the cause of Christ that was about to be won. "Imagine how many kids we're going to reach," they said. "This will be an outpouring of the Holy Spirit like we haven't seen in years." I quickly found myself caught up in the excitement, and I worked harder than ever on my presentation, praying that God's message would flow through me.

But somehow, as the date for the concert drew near, the dynamics began to change. The promoters were talking more about the potential profits to be made than they were about the kids we were trying to reach. Everyone was lining up for a share of the financial pie.

Attendance was even greater than we'd expected, and the night of the festival many had to be turned away at the door. As I stood to speak to a capacity crowd of well over twenty thousand people, I felt the power of the Holy Spirit. I was given much less time to speak than I had anticipated, but I wanted the words to count. I began by sharing my testimony, telling of the hopelessness and violence and poverty that Jesus had saved me from. Then I pleaded for every lost person in the audience to accept Jesus as Lord. I poured every ounce of myself into the message, hoping to reach some lost kids for Christ.

I'd been told that logistics and time didn't allow for an altar call, so when I finished speaking, I was quickly led off the stage and into a room in the back. "Good job, Nicky," they said as we walked. "You really touched them."

"Ladies and gentleman," I heard the announcer shouting into the microphone, "let's hear it for Nicky Cruz!" The audience responded with loud applause. Meanwhile I looked back to see a music band running up on stage, followed by a popular Christian singer. The crowd went wild. The music started up as the performer began to sing and run back and forth across the stage, whipping the crowd into a frenzy.

One after the other, more entertainers took to the stage and played their music. Each time the audience went crazy with excitement. A lot of money was made that night, especially through T-shirt and CD sales, and the concert was considered a wild success. But somehow I felt empty and cold.

That night, as I lay in bed, physically and emotionally exhausted, a sick feeling crept into my heart and mind. *Is this what I was called to do?* I thought. *Is this the way God wants to use me? Did I really help anyone tonight? Did they even hear what I said?*

I'm honestly not against Christian entertainment, and I enjoy Christian music as much as anyone. It plays an important role in the body of Christ. But when the gospel of Jesus starts to become lost in commercialization, we stand in real danger of losing our perspective, often perverting the very message we're called to share.

I saw that happening in many circles within Christianity—and still do. In my travels through the years, I've seen many good preachers and evangelists begin watering down the gospel in an effort to appeal to the greatest number of people. "God wants you to be wealthy," they say with conviction. "If you accept him, he guarantees to make you happy and rich." Of course, one of the prerequisites of this promise is to give generously and regularly to their particular ministries.

There will always be those who preach a different gospel and those who use ministry for their own personal gain. It would be naive to believe otherwise. But the excesses I saw were becoming more disturbing by the day.

A STRANGE PATH FOR *RUN BABY RUN*

It would be great if people in Christian ministry would always rise above the greed that so permeates our society, but that's simply not the case. People are easily influenced by money and power and can often let you down, especially if they stand to profit in the process. I learned that lesson early in my ministry.

Following the success of David Wilkerson's powerful book *The Cross and the Switchblade* (which chronicled his ministry to inner-city gangs in New York and his struggle to lead me to Christ), a small publishing house approached me with the idea of putting my story in book form as well. After interviewing five writers, I chose one I felt I could work with best, and the publisher drafted a shared-royalty agreement between the two of us. I knew almost nothing about the publishing business, so I trusted the publisher to guide the process and protect my interests. He continued to tell me not to worry, that he would take care of everything.

None of us expected the book—*Run Baby Run*—to become the publishing phenomenon that it did. Released in hardcover, it soon rose to the bestseller list. A paperback edition was quickly released, and that's when sales went through the roof. It wasn't long before a million copies had been sold (the total today, still climbing, is more than twelve million). Meanwhile, I've always known that God put his anointing on this book—just as he has on my personal testimony—because it's honest and compelling enough to change hearts and lead people to Christ. I've never assumed any credit.

But when books sell well, a lot of money begins changing hands, and greed can easily creep into the mix. I had received no initial advance payment of royalties, and despite the book's quick success, I received only a few royalty checks during the first three years after its release. The publisher continued to make excuses for this fact, telling me that they were having trouble tracking sales and that most of my profit would be coming later, after they recovered their costs of publication. (I later discovered that the entire initial advance, which was rather large, had been given to my cowriter. I've never blamed my cowriter for this fact; I'm sure he thought it was simply part of my original agreement with the publisher.)

One day I received a letter that the publishing house had filed for bankruptcy. I wasn't sure how this was going to affect my book contract, and I was always unable to find anyone to tell me. I was busy with my ministry, so I didn't worry much about it. Ten years went by before I heard anything. During that time, the book continued to be regularly reprinted under five or six different publishers' labels. I knew sales were good, since it consistently appeared on bestseller lists, but still I was receiving no royalties.

I discussed this problem with my cowriter, who was as confused as I was. It was clear that a lot of money was changing hands, but somehow we were being left out of the loop. Then one day, almost out of the blue, I received a small royalty check, the first in a decade. There was no explanation about the lack of communication over the years or about money owed for back royalties. When we looked into the matter, we found that almost all of the past sales records had been lost or at least made unavailable.

It was obvious that we were being taken advantage of, but I never wanted to push the issue. God was using my book to introduce millions to the gospel, and that was all the payment I really needed. Still, it bothered me greatly to know how much money was being diverted from the hands of our ministry to a handful of opportunists, corrupted by greed. And, quite honestly, it was happening at a time when I really could have used the money. Full-time evangelism, though gratifying, is not the best paying profession, and I had a family to feed and four daughters to put through college. Still, I never wanted to make an issue of money, so I consistently let the matter drop.

In spite of these bizarre circumstances, in spite of the greed and manipulation that has plagued the publishing of *Run Baby Run* since the beginning, God has continued to use the book for his glory. Millions of people have been brought to Jesus as a direct result of it. Moreover, the success of that book is largely responsible for the high visibility God has given my life and ministry, allowing me to do even greater things in his name. Even in the midst of man's sin and weakness, God's glory shines through!

GOD'S REPRIMAND?

There were other concerns as well that plagued me during this period of my life. I've long since put many of these matters behind me, and it isn't necessary to reveal them in detail, but at the time they weighed painfully on my spirit.

In so many ways during those years I felt I was being used within the Christian "industry," often by people I loved and respected. My story is a unique and compelling one, and my presence at an event would often attract a decent crowd. I was seen as something of a novelty—the gangster from *The Cross and the Switchblade* film, the "gang leader turned preacher." People began to see me as an opportunity to draw more attention to their own ministry or event—and larger audiences meant bigger offerings.

Within churches and evangelistic circles I also sensed a great deal of prejudice against both my nationality and my ministry. It was seldom obvious or overt but more of an underlying lack of respect, a subtle condescension. I didn't fit into the mold of the average Christian speaker, I had my own way of doing things, and my mission was to the inner city, to the lepers of our day, to the people whom many Christians don't want to believe exist.

So many times I had to close my eyes to the prejudice among the Christian community. I learned to look instead to Jesus for the love and help I needed, but it always hurt to feel like such an outsider among my own people.

On top of all this, our ministry had been dealing with a number of internal struggles. We discovered that our bookkeeper was siphoning funds from our account. The amount she took was rather substantial, and the revelation was devastating to me. I trusted this woman and considered her a friend. The thought that she would steal from us was almost more than I could bear.

Gloria and I had been so busy we hadn't had time to watch what was going on. Besides raising our family, for seventeen years we managed a home for male juvenile delinquents. These boys were often so needy and lost—usually unwanted drug addicts and runaways—and it took all the energy we could muster to meet their daily emotional and physical needs, while almost every weekend I would be on the road speaking. Our bookkeeper took advantage of our busy schedules and our trust and used the opportunity for personal gain.

Through that revelation we were forced to dismiss a couple of other people from our staff, leaving our office desperately short-handed and in disarray. For a while it took all our time and energy to bring order out of the chaos. Meanwhile we interviewed numerous applicants for the vacant positions, yet continued to feel uneasy about the people applying. In spite of our prayers, God wasn't bringing the right people to our doorstep.

At times I wondered if our ministry wasn't under the hand of God's discipline and reprimand. I knew we were under attack by Satan—we always had been—but was God trying to send us a message as well? Was he trying to tell me it was time to close our doors and leave this work to another person or ministry?

SOMETHING HAS TO CHANGE

Such were the frustrations and disappointments that had been building within me for years, leaving me weary and ready to quit the ministry. All this was the background to my thoughts on that long morning jog on a dusty road in

Mexico. God knew my heart, and that's why he sent a messenger to my aid just when I needed it most, instilling me with fresh fervency.

I'm continually humbled to remember the precious gift of that personally delivered message from God that morning—the confirmation of my life's work and God's mandate for me to continue. I'll never be able to fully express my appreciation—the words of a dozen books wouldn't be enough to describe the joy and wonder and fresh sense of purpose that this new anointing breathed into my soul and spirit, rekindling my passion.

God had placed a fresh calling on my life—the calling to continue in ministry to the lost. That message was perfectly clear. Yet somehow I knew in my heart I couldn't continue on the same path I'd been traveling. Something would have to change.

I felt in my spirit that God had a new direction for my outreach ministry, but he had yet to reveal to me what that direction was and where it would take me.

That piece of this divine puzzle was about to unfold—not through more angelic visits but through the holy and faithful fire of his Spirit's guiding light.

❧

unpredictable, uncontrollable

God has continued to show me that the Holy Spirit's fire isn't something we can calculate or control, either in how he motivates and guides us or in how he works in the lives of others through our ministry and our serving others. When we ignore the Spirit's nudging and leading, when we try to do things on our own instead of listening for his direction, we often miss out on the best and glorious plans he has in store for us.

But it can be hard to follow the Spirit's leadings, because he's so unpredictable.

WHEN IT DOESN'T MAKE SENSE

In the eighth chapter of Acts, an angel of the Lord told Philip to stop what he was doing and start out toward the road between Jerusalem and Gaza. At the time Philip was busy preaching and healing in Samaria, doing mighty works for the Lord. Philip no doubt had a number of things to do and probably wondered why the Lord would want to interrupt such a powerful time in his ministry. The Lord gave Philip no explanation, and he had no idea why he was being sent. Yet he obeyed.

While traveling down this road, Philip was passed by a chariot. The Spirit spoke to him, telling him to stay near it. He caught up to the chariot and heard a man inside reading from Isaiah the prophet. The man was a eunuch from Ethiopia, an important official of the queen. Immediately Philip understood why the Spirit had led him to this place in the middle of nowhere. He was able to witness to the eunuch and bring him to Christ (8:26-35).

Had Philip not been listening to the Spirit's leading, or had he chosen not to heed his direction (or worse yet, failed to acknowledge that the Spirit actually speaks to us), he would have missed out on this divine appointment.

The truth is, had Philip stayed in Samaria preaching, he probably would have reached many more for Christ during this period of time. Instead, God diverted him for the sake of one soul. It would have been easy for Philip to question this mandate, to second-guess God's wisdom in leading him away during a successful and busy time in his outreach, but he didn't. Philip understood God's authority and knew better than to question his ways.

What does it mean to trust God and walk in the Spirit? Jesus offers us a perfect description: "The wind blows wherever it pleases. You hear its sound, but you cannot tell where it comes from or where it is going. *So it is with everyone born of the Spirit*" (John 3:8).

When and where God leads may not always make sense to us. In fact, usually it doesn't. But a true disciple learns to listen and obey, regardless of his or her own opinions or agenda at the moment.

Sadly, too many Christians today are so busy with the daily chores of living that they've left no room for the Spirit's guidance. Even when the Lord does get a message through, they have to first see if they can fit it into their daily calendar. We've left almost no room for God to work and move and anoint us with his power. And people are going hungry for Christ's healing touch because of it.

LIMITING GOD

Not long ago I was watching a television evangelist teach on the working of the Holy Spirit. He began by exploring the many attributes of the Holy Spirit we see in Scripture—the powerful ways he worked in the lives of biblical characters and the ways he's described by Jesus and the gospel writers. It was an encouraging exercise. I love hearing about the glorious dimensions of God's power on earth.

But then this evangelist used those attributes to make a list of what the Holy Spirit can and can't do among us. He noted the ways that we can expect to see the Spirit's power in our lives, then listed the limitations God has put on him—the ways that we should *not* expect to see him work. At one point he even said that the Holy Spirit is under our submission and can work only when we release him to do so. According to this evangelist, the Holy Spirit can do no more or less than we choose to allow.

I couldn't believe my ears. Here was this man, a preacher of the gospel, trying to educate the Holy Spirit on his job description! And people all over his congregation were taking careful notes so that they, too, would be able to keep the Holy Spirit in line.

To me this is more than just an error in interpretation; this is man trying to limit God—trying to tell the Creator how to run his creation. And that's a dangerous thing to do, to teach, or to believe. The truth is, God's Spirit is going to work however and whenever he pleases, regardless of what we think or believe. And when he does, it will seldom come in the way we expect.

A YOUNG MAN, HIS RAT, AND GLORIA

When we allow the Spirit freedom to work—we can be in for plenty of surprises.

For example, I remember one particular crusade we had in London. It was a number of years ago, when the British economy was suffering and drugs and alcohol had become a huge problem among their young people. In this environment, the people were spiritually open. We rented the only available venue. It held only seventeen hundred, but we packed it out each night, turning numbers of people away at the door.

I still travel to England several times a year to minister, and it never ceases to amaze me how hungry the people are for the gospel and God's word. Many pastors and evangelists are surprised when they hear me say that; England has a reputation as a godless land filled with old, ornate churches and cathedrals that in generations past were filled on Sunday mornings but now are mostly empty. It's true that many in England have lost their roots of faith. Still, what I see when I go there is a country filled with lost and hurting souls, desperately longing for hope. And for some reason, God has given me a special bond with them. Our meetings regularly pack some of the largest auditoriums in the major cities—London, Manchester, Birmingham, Liverpool—as well as in smaller cities and suburbs. We reach not only the inner city but also middle-class and wealthy neighborhoods. My book *Run Baby Run* has been a perennial bestseller in England, and readers there seem to identify deeply with my story—not so much with the poverty and violence I suffered, but with the hopelessness and despair I felt in the midst of it.

On the opening night of that London crusade years ago, the crowd that gathered was a diverse one—hippies, punk rockers, addicts, Goths, hookers, homeless people, and more. Everywhere I looked were kids with purple, green, and orange hair, usually spiked high in the air. Most were wearing black clothes emblazoned with satanic symbols, and their bodies were pierced in just about every place imaginable. Chains were dangling everywhere. I'd never seen so many confused and broken kids.

This particular night, Gloria had a seat on the front row of the auditorium. While I was preparing to go on stage, I looked over in her direction and saw a young man sit down next to her. He looked frightening—a Goth with all the trimmings. As he shifted to one side, I noticed something crawling over his lap. I looked intently and realized it was a black rat on a small leash.

If you knew Gloria, you'd understand why this scene was so interesting. Gloria is terrified of mice. She's not just afraid of them, mind you; she is petrified at the sight of them.

At first she didn't notice, and I hoped against hope it would remain that way. But when he turned his head away from her, I saw her eyes glance in his direction, just in time to see the rat shuffle. She froze stiff in a daze of terror, her eyes as wide as saucers. I prayed that she would keep her composure.

Eventually she gave a panic-stricken glance in my direction. I knew what she was trying to tell me with her eyes, though she didn't have to say a word: *Nicky, do something! You know I can't deal with this. You have to ask him to leave, or take his rat out of here—whatever it takes to get me away from this horrible creature!*

Gloria knows I love her and would never let anything happen to her, but I wasn't about to kick a person out of a crusade, especially someone who so obviously needed the Lord. When a person takes the initiative not only to attend one of my events but to sit on the front row, there's a reason for it. The Holy Spirit was obviously orchestrating something powerful in his life, and it wasn't my job to question it.

I motioned for her to just stay calm. *It will all be over soon,* I tried to signal her. *Just relax and nothing will happen to you.* I'm not sure she got the message, but she remained in her seat, stiff as a board through the entire event. She was quite a trooper.

Later, during the altar call, this young man was the first person to step forward and receive Christ. He stood down front with his rat in one hand and his bowed head in the other, with tears rolling down the side of his face, as a volunteer worker laid hands on him and led him in a prayer of repentance.

CONFRONTING TWO HECKLERS

During another crusade in England just a few months later, the same dynamic was taking shape. The audience was filled with punk rockers and Goths, two of whom sat on the front row. They'd been drinking and were intoxicated. They seemed to be there for their own enjoyment, and while I was sharing my testimony, they laughed and heckled and generally tried to disrupt the event. I tried ignoring them, but the distraction only got worse.

That night the Spirit told me to do something I never dreamed I would do. In the middle of my talk I stopped and told the audience I would have to leave the stage for a few minutes. "Just bear with me," I said. "There's something I need to take care of."

I walked off the stage and made my way to where those two young men were sitting, then bent down before them. "I know you two think this is a joke, but I came here to talk about Jesus, and the rest of these people came here to listen." They leaned back in their chairs and got very quiet, somewhat stunned by my actions.

"I'm not asking you to leave. In fact, I'm commanding you to stay. Because I know something that you don't. The reason you're laughing is because you're nervous. Inside you're afraid, because Satan has got a hold on your hearts. But tonight Jesus is going to do something in your life—something you never expected. Something that will change your life forever."

They sat looking at me without moving a muscle. I knew I had their attention.

"I'm no longer going to put up with your laughing and heckling," I continued. "I want you to sit quietly while I finish. Then, if you still feel like it, you can make all the jokes you want at my expense. But right now, you sit still, shut up, and listen to my testimony."

I made my way back on stage and continued where I'd left off. The two didn't say a word through the remainder of my talk, but during the altar call, one of them quickly came forward to stand at the front of the auditorium. He was weeping with repentance and asked for prayer.

It's wise not to second-guess the Spirit when he's moving and working in the lives of lost souls.

GOD'S NEXT MESSAGE FOR MY FUTURE

Those types of experiences were pretty common to me whenever I ministered in England. That's one of the reasons God has continued to send me there on such a regular basis. And perhaps that's why he chose to use England as the place where he would communicate his next message to me regarding his vision for my future, just a few months after my miraculous encounter in Mexico with one of God's angels.

It happened during another powerful outreach crusade. Gloria was again with me on this trip, and we'd been praying that God would flow his Spirit through us. We'd also been praying fervently for a sense of God's new direction for our ministry.

One night, after our crusade meeting that evening, we grabbed a quick bite to eat and went back to our hotel room. It was late, and we were looking forward to a good night's sleep. We washed up, changed for bed, then decided to spend a few minutes unwinding by catching the news on the television.

During the broadcast, we saw a special report on the United States, uncovering the hate and violence running rampant within the schools, neighborhoods, and streets of our inner cities and suburbs. It was an eye-opening experience to witness my homeland through the eyes of another country—to see us the way they see us.

British television content isn't censored as much as television in America is, so there was very little they didn't show. It was the most graphic and bloody news program I'd ever witnessed. We sat in horror as the reporters exposed in full color the violence and cruelty ravaging the streets of our cities. I began to understand why so few English people showed a desire to travel to our country. If you didn't know better, you'd think we were a huge Third World nation filled with nothing but hostility and hatred.

Over and over we saw scenes of fights and riots, of addicts shooting up in the streets, of runaway teens selling themselves on busy street corners, of kids killing kids without regard or remorse. We saw fires and looting in the streets, policemen in riot gear getting pummeled by masses of angry teens and adults, filth and debris littering the sidewalks on every corner.

Gloria and I found it hard to watch. It had been more than thirty years since I had lived on the streets, running with a violent street gang, and I'd seen more than my share of blood and hate. But even then I didn't remember seeing anything quite like this. I'd spent most of my life working with kids in the inner city, and I knew that things in America were not as rosy and clean as most people liked to believe. But somehow, seeing the aggression and brutality in such graphic detail served to underscore the extent of the problem.

Gloria turned to me with disgust in her eyes.

"Nicky, what's wrong with our country?" she said. "Are things this bad in the U.S.?"

"I guess they are," I answered. "I don't want to believe it, but somehow things are only getting worse. For all our efforts, there are still a lot of people who need the Lord."

As we sat and watched, numbed by the horror of the images, God began speaking to me in an undeniable way. It wasn't an audible voice, but the message was clear.

Nicky, he said, *pay attention to what I'm showing you. This is your calling. This is where you belong. I saved you from a life of hate and violence in the United States, and I called you to minister to the people you left behind. These are the people who will listen to you. They trust you because you know what they're going through. I want you to go back to the United States, back to the streets, back to your roots, and save my people from the darkness. I'm calling you as my missionary to the inner cities.*

Forget those people who use you and want to make you a celebrity. And stop focusing on those who are already saved. Let me do that. I want you to go back where you started, to the people who need you most. Take my message of forgiveness to the streets, and I will show my power and strength to them in ways they can never forget or deny.

MY STORY—ONLY FOR GOD'S GLORY

This was a mandate from God every bit as clear as the one I had received as a young man, more than thirty years earlier, when God called me to work with David Wilkerson as the first director of Teen Challenge, a ministry to young people in New York. That calling later expanded and grew into a national and international outreach program.

Through the years, as my ministry had grown, so had my level of influence. I was called on to speak to larger gatherings, to share my vision with the body of Christ, and to write books and articles about my views and experiences. My books sold well and my testimony moved people, so my demand as a speaker grew even greater and my schedule grew busier along with it. The change was a gradual and unplanned one. I never signed on to be a public figure and a Christian celebrity; I was simply forced into that role.

But now God was calling me back to my roots, back into the street ministry where I started. And he was promising to go before me with an even greater level of authority and might.

On that night in our hotel room in England, God completed his message with one last word of admonishment in my spirit. *From now on your testimony is for the lost and helpless, not for the indulgence of the saved. Your story is to be used to bring people to me. Never again cheapen my touch on your life by using it for the entertainment of others. Remember your past and continue to tell your story, but only for my glory. And for the sake of those caught in a web of violence and anger.*

Gloria and I spent much of that night in prayer. As I told her of the mandate God had placed on my heart and spirit, I could tell it was a bittersweet message for her to hear. Though we both committed to go wherever God wanted us, there was a small part of us that had been looking forward to slowing down and moving on to other things. It was a night of both joy and mourning. We were happy to have been given a clear new focus for our ministry, but we were sad that our dreams of retirement were being put on hold.

This wasn't an easy pill to swallow for either of us. Still, we were excited to see where this new directive would lead and how God's hand would be reshaping our lives and our ministry.

A SOBERING FAMILY MOMENT

When we arrived back home, one of the first things we did was call our children together for a family meeting. I wondered how they would receive this news. My kids knew I had been considering moving out of public ministry, and they were looking forward to more time together, even dreaming aloud about all the things we were going to do with my extra time. Alicia, my oldest daughter, and her husband, Patrick, had been working for my ministry for a few years, and I knew they were already considering moving into a new career field.

With the family gathered, Gloria and I told them of the television broadcast we'd seen and the level of hate and hostility that exploded on the screen before us. We told them of our new mandate from God and his directive for me to continue in my ministry, refocusing on inner-city evangelism.

We were all well aware of the inevitable dangers this new vision from God would place on my life. Just a few days earlier a news story had run about a soldier who had been shot in the streets of an urban neighborhood. He'd survived several years in the military, even a stint on the front lines of the Persian Gulf War, but two days after returning home from that service he was killed in the streets of a local neighborhood. Those types of reports were becoming a common occurrence.

"This is a violent time in our world," I said, "more violent than I think it has ever been. Our urban neighborhoods have turned into war zones, and this will not be an easy time for any of us. But God has always protected me, and he will continue to do so. As long as he's by my side, I have no reason to fear."

Several of my children began to tear up as I spoke. "I'm aware that you're probably disappointed, but this is something I have to do. I hope you all understand that. God has made that decision for me. All I'm asking from you is your prayers and blessings as I embark on this new mission."

We sat silently for a moment as the news sunk in. It was a sobering moment for the Cruz family.

CONFIRMATION OF GOD'S CALL

Suddenly Alicia stood up and walked over to my chair, placing her hand on my shoulder, tears running down the sides of her face. "Daddy, Patrick and I have been praying for months for God to show us his direction for our future. We've both felt him calling us to work in inner-city ministry. We haven't talked about it with you and mom because we thought you were going to retire. Now I know that he wants us to continue working with you. We could help you refocus your ministry."

Her words took me by surprise. I thought she and Patrick were looking forward to moving on, and I didn't want them to feel obligated to stay with me. I looked at Patrick to see him nodding in confirmation.

"We'll do this together," Alicia said as she bent down to hug me.

My daughter Nicole spoke up next. "I want to help you too," she said through tears. "Whatever you need, you know I'm here to help."

Laura and Elena, my two other daughters, spoke almost in unison, "We're with you too, Daddy. We've always been with you."

I struggled to keep my composure. Hearing my family's confirmation of God's calling brought more joy than I ever imagined.

Gloria stood and gathered us all in a tight circle. "Nicky, if God has called you, he's called us as well. We're your family, and we're all in this together. From now on this will be a family ministry. We'll do it together. We're not afraid. God will protect us just like he's always watched over you.

"The kids are almost grown, and there's no reason I can't travel with you wherever you go. We can help you take care of the office and your schedule.

We'll share the duties. Imagine how God can use us as a family, working together in his service. The devil won't know what hit him!"

It was an emotional time for us all. We spent the next hour hugging and praying and crying and laughing together, praising God for this new chapter in the life of our family. Our fears and reservations had suddenly turned to excitement and anticipation. We began to dream aloud of the powerful new ways God would be using us.

I pulled my family close and began to pray.

"Sweet Jesus, you are so good to us. We love you, Jesus. And we're ready for whatever you want us to do. Breathe your Spirit into ours as we move into this new empowering. Anoint us with your glory and your might.

"Precious Jesus, go with us as we brave the dangers of the inner cities. We know you are with us, and we have no fear. Now guide us, Lord. Wherever you lead, we will follow. Together we will burst through the gates of hell and snatch your precious treasures out of the mouth of Satan. Rain your power upon our lives. Flow your love through us.

"Jesus, keep us together with one vision, and keep us strong!"

TRUCE

When God eight years ago intervened in my ministry in this way—calling me to a renewed vision and direction for an outreach to the inner cities—I knew I was in for an exciting ride. And by calling my entire family into that ministry with me, he revitalized my heart and soul in a way I could never have expected.

Since then, my family has worked closely by my side in every aspect of our outreach. Gloria travels with me regularly, Patrick and Alicia work full-time for the ministry, and my other three daughters and their husbands help in our crusades whenever possible. God also restructured our office staff and has continued to bring to us some of the best, most dedicated workers and volunteers that our ministry has ever seen. Today I'm finally able to relax and focus on evangelism, trusting my family and new staff to take care of the daily details. It's a welcome change.

In the beginning we called our outreach ministry Save Our City, but a few years ago we began to use the name TRUCE, an acronym developed by my daughter Alicia that stands for "To Reach Urban Children Everywhere." It's a perfect fit for what we do.

From the start I determined that things were going to be different with my speaking and traveling schedule. Today churches know that I will go out of my way to make an appearance and speak in their assemblies, but only if they're serious about wanting to reach out to their community. I let them know that my message will be confrontational and hard-hitting, with a call for repentance afterward. If a church is looking for someone to bring a simple, nonthreatening message to their congregation, I usually decline and refer them to someone else. But if they're committed to reaching the lost, maybe even agreeing to bring in some kids from a detention center or a local shelter or spending a few days knocking on doors and inviting their neighbors to come, they can count on me to be there.

The truth is, if I have to decide between ministering to a dozen gang members on a street corner or a stadium filled with ten thousand saved Christians, I'll choose the street corner anytime, because that's what God has called me to do.

We also committed our new outreach to other changes. During previous years I had served mostly as a celebrity speaker, brought in to help draw crowds to events planned by Christian celebrities and media organizations. Most of these events were one-night stands. I seldom got the opportunity to build relationships with the lost or with new believers, to engage in personal, long-term ministry, or to be involved in the follow-up strategy. Now we wanted more than that. We wanted to develop a long-term love affair with the people and the cities we reached out to.

Today, when the Spirit leads us to evangelize a city, we partner with a few local churches both in the inner city and suburban areas. We set dates for a final three- or four-day run in a local auditorium or stadium of a dramatic production of *Run Baby Run,* which we've developed as the heart of our ministry. We then spend six months prior to that event reaching out to the community, getting to know the people in the inner-city neighborhoods. We organize with local churches, soliciting their help with street evangelism and various publicity and promotional efforts.

Several evenings a week, for three weeks before the drama production, we take our hit-and-run outreaches to the streets. In the final week these hit-and-runs are held nightly. We use this opportunity to introduce people to the believers and the churches in their area that can help them. We pass out free tickets to the stage production and encourage everyone to come.

Although the *Run Baby Run* stage production gets most of the attention both from the media and the Christian community, it's our street outreaches, our hit-and-run curbside concerts, that seem to cut to the core of inner cities most effectively. It's our way of meeting and ministering to people where they live, in their homes and neighborhoods. Instead of inviting them to a church service to learn about God, we take the Holy Spirit right to their doorstep. We introduce them to God on their turf, not ours. And by doing so, we're able to reach people who otherwise might never have the chance to hear about Jesus.

CHAPTER FIVE

The spirit's Detours

I often wonder how Jesus' life would have looked if he'd allowed his disciples to set his schedule for him. What if he'd appointed John or Peter or Matthew as his ministry coordinator? They probably would have taken the role seriously, drawn up a tight schedule, and made sure Jesus was on time and in the right outfit for each occasion.

But Jesus didn't do it that way. He traveled wherever the Spirit led, ministering, healing, teaching, or retreating as God led him. He refused to be bound by a rigid and predetermined schedule. His life was filled with detours.

THE RIGHT TIME

Once, when Jesus traveled from Judea to Galilee, the apostle John records that "he had to go through Samaria" (John 4:4). The fact is, Jesus didn't *have* to go through Samaria to get to Galilee, geographically speaking. In fact, because Jews hated Samaritans, Jews regularly took the long way around in order to avoid that region. But Jesus felt compelled to go through Samaria because that's where the Spirit now led him—he had to go through Samaria not as a matter of geography, but as a matter of mission, out of obedience to the Spirit's guidance.

When he reached Samaria he sent his disciples on ahead of him and sat down beside Jacob's well. There he waited for his divine encounter with the Samaritan woman, where he supernaturally discerned everything about her. Their conversation changed her life forever, and she became the world's first evangelist, witnessing about Jesus to the people of her city. Jesus stayed with these Samaritans for two more days and was able to bring many others to salvation before moving on. This encounter would never have happened if Jesus hadn't been following the Spirit's leading.

Later, in Galilee, as the time for the Jewish Feast of Tabernacles in Jerusalem drew near, the brothers of Jesus urged him to travel there "so that your disciples may see the miracles you do. No one who wants to become a public figure acts in secret. Since you are doing these things, show yourself to the world" (John 7:3-4).

But Jesus was on a different schedule. He answered them, "You go to the Feast. I am not yet going up to this Feast, because for me *the right time* has not yet come" (7:8).

Once again Jesus was waiting for clearance from the Holy Spirit to move. He was waiting for the right time to make an entrance at the Feast and to reveal his wisdom and teaching to the people in Jerusalem. He knew, in fact, that he *was* the true feast—the Messiah they'd been waiting for. He himself was the reason for their celebration, though they did not realize it.

BIG FAT PIGS

Another time, when Jesus was traveling by boat with his disciples (Mark 5:1-18), he took them across the Sea of Galilee to the region of Gerasenes, a land inhabited by Gentiles. When Jesus got out of the boat, a demon-possessed man ran toward him and fell to his knees. The demons shouted at Jesus, "What do you want with me, Jesus, Son of the Most High God?" The demons begged him to have mercy on them.

Jesus asked the man, "What is your name?" But his answer came again from the demons within him: "My name is Legion, for we are many."

A herd of pigs was feeding nearby, and the demons begged Jesus to allow them to enter into the animals. The demons knew that they had no authority and power in the presence of God's glory. Satan loves to taunt and ridicule helpless people, but when Jesus shows up, the devil quickly turns into the weak and pathetic loser he really is. That's another aspect of life that hasn't changed. Only today, Satan is forced to cower and hide not just at the sight of Jesus but of any follower of Christ. The name of Jesus in the mouth of a believer has awesome power.

Giving the demons permission to enter into the body of a bunch of nasty pigs was a fitting irony, and Jesus let them do it. At once the pigs plunged off a nearby cliff to their deaths. To me, this has always seemed a perfect foreshadowing of what Satan and his demons have to look forward to on the Day of Judgment.

While we're on the subject, have you ever wondered why pigs walk with their heads down toward the ground? I've never seen a pig that would look you in the eye, and I'm guessing you haven't either. What are they so embarrassed about? They're embarrassed because their mother is a big fat pig. And now—thanks to Jesus—Satan, too, is nothing more than a big fat pig!

After that encounter, Jesus and his disciples got into their boat and headed back out. The only discernible reason for their stop was the beckoning of the Holy Spirit. Jesus was willing to take a long detour for the sake of one demon-possessed man.

If only we believers today could put away our own schedules and agendas and be willing to move as the Spirit guides us—to take detours!

I thank God that David Wilkerson was willing to do that. I was just a wild and lost nineteen-year-old brutalizing the streets of New York when he obeyed the Spirit's leading and came to preach in the same streets. He left a pregnant bride at home alone to make the trip and risked his neck coming onto my turf. But his conviction and obedience to God's gentle whisper was unwavering. If it weren't for his willingness to take that detour, today I would probably be dead or serving a life sentence in prison. I owe the healing of my life and soul to David's faithfulness before God.

Pray for God to lead you to those who need his saving grace, then follow when he does. Be willing to take detours for the sake of Jesus.

AFTER AN EARTHQUAKE, HEALING

As God has continued to go before me with authority, with each new experience of his surprising guidance in our ministry he has instilled in me an even greater level of trust and boldness. I've discovered how far God is willing to go to draw a lost soul to himself.

I've walked by faith and trusted the Spirit's leading, and God has been gracious to reveal his supernatural power in our ministry. We never knew what God was going to do next. The Holy Spirit was in control; we just tried to follow his lead and minister however and whenever he wanted.

In 1985 we held a crusade in Mexico City just a few weeks after a devastating earthquake that left much of the city in ruins. We considered canceling the long-planned event and wondered if we would even be allowed to hold it, but God paved the way and beckoned us to forge ahead. We knew this disaster would either draw people toward God or cause them to turn against him, but we didn't know which. The people of the city had been so demoralized by this tragedy, and so many were affected, that we honestly didn't expect many to come. But they proved us wrong; more than fourteen thousand people packed into the stadium for the first night of the crusade.

God's Spirit was so real that night that we could feel his presence. The Holy Spirit flowed through me as I shared my testimony, raining conviction on the crowd. I could feel the power. I knew that many were ready to accept Jesus as their Savior, but just as I started to make a call for repentance, God decided to turn the evening into a healing service.

It started when a mother brought her deaf and dumb little daughter forward and asked one of the volunteers to pray over her. For the first time in her life the girl started to speak. Her first word was "Jesus." The mother screamed with excitement, bouncing up and down in front of the stage area. It took me a few moments to realize what had happened. It had nothing to do with me; I was just as confused as everyone else. But when the crowd saw what God had done, they went crazy with excitement.

Just then another woman made her way to the front. Her spine was so deformed and misshapen that she couldn't even lift her head. She walked hunched over, with her eyes to the ground. At her request, another worker laid hands on her and prayed for healing, and she slowly began to straighten. Within minutes she was standing upright, weeping uncontrollably with joy.

I was so taken aback by the whole thing that I wasn't sure what to do. I'm an evangelist, a minister of the gospel, not a faith healer. I'm used to praying for people's souls, not their afflictions. My unchanging message is the healing of the soul, and that's the greatest miracle. But this night, God decided to heal bodies, so that's what we did.

The next person to come forward was a large man who lifted his shirt to expose a huge lump protruding from the side of his stomach. It was a tumor the size of a soccer ball. Several workers began praying over him, and we all watched in amazement as the growth shrank then disappeared right before our eyes. If there was even a hint of doubt that these miraculous healings were genuine and from God, it was completely dispelled at that moment.

After that I made a call for anyone who was sick and in need of healing to stand where they were, then asked believers around them to pray and lay hands on them. Throughout the auditorium people were shouting and screaming in joy as God's Spirit came down to heal and minister. We lost count of all the people who found healing during that service.

More than a thousand came forward to receive Christ that night. After seeing what God had done, the crowd was left with no other explanation. We were all eyewitnesses to his power.

A PERSISTENT MOTHER

On another occasion I was scheduled to speak at a large church in Brooklyn. It happened in 1962, early in my ministry as an evangelist, and I was still somewhat fresh in my Christian faith. A few hours before the service, I was in my office at Teen Challenge praying and preparing for my talk, when suddenly the phone rang. It was a young woman from the area. She said, "Mr. Cruz, I know that you're speaking tonight, and I wanted you to know that I'm bringing my seven-year-old daughter to the service. She's been crippled since birth, and I want you to pray for her."

As I listened I tried to think of a polite way to explain to the woman that I'm not a faith healer, that my ministry is one of evangelism. "I don't mind praying for your daughter," I told her, "but I don't want to get your hopes up. I'm planning to preach about Jesus and salvation tonight, and I don't want you to be hurt if your daughter doesn't get healed."

She persisted. "I plan to be there tonight," she said firmly, "and I want you to pray for my daughter."

Again I told her I'd be happy to pray for her daughter, but I continued to caution her that healing wasn't part of my ministry—or my calling. After a long conversation she finally hung up, and I got back to my studies.

Not long afterward the phone rang again. "I'm just calling to remind you again," the woman's voice said, "that I plan to be there tonight, and I really need you to pray for my daughter. I know you don't think you can heal her—but I know you can. I'll be looking for you, and I want you to be watching for me."

This time my reply was a bit more curt and forceful. I once again conveyed my willingness to pray for her daughter, but I explained that she shouldn't get her hopes up.

The woman responded by telling me what she'd be wearing that night so I could pick her out in the crowd, adding again that she would be looking for me.

As I hung up the phone I knew I would do everything I could to avoid this woman at the service. She was so forceful that I was convinced she would simply make a scene and embarrass both of us during the altar call. I even began to pray she would somehow not make it to the meeting.

When I arrived at the church, well in advance of the service, I was thrilled to see that the place was completely packed out with a line of people trailing down the street. I remember praying, *Thank you, God, for filling up the building so quickly. I'm sure this woman won't be able to make her way into the auditorium with a crippled daughter, and I won't have to deal with her.* It was a selfish prayer, but I was convinced the woman would simply make a scene in front of everyone if I were forced to try to heal her daughter.

I happily took my place near the front of the auditorium and waited through the music and announcements. When it was time for me to speak, I made my way up the aisle and toward the pulpit. Just before reaching it, I looked to my left and saw the woman waving her arms frantically, trying to get my attention. She was seated on the third row, with her crippled daughter by her side. My heart sank. *Dear God,* I prayed. *Please help me know how to deal with this.*

My sermon that night was on the love of God and the hope of salvation, and afterward people from every corner of the auditorium began making their way toward the front in repentance. Everywhere I looked people were crying and begging for prayers and forgiveness. It was a powerful evening of conviction and rejoicing. As I was praying for these people, I saw the woman standing in line before me with her little daughter beside her. A deacon was holding the poor girl up in his arms as the woman pushed her way through the crowd toward the front.

As she reached the stage area, the woman looked up at me with hope burning in her eyes. "Mr. Cruz," she said, "I'm the woman who called you today. Please pray for my daughter."

I was so nervous that my first reaction was to turn to the church's pastor standing beside me and ask him if he would pray for the girl. He looked at me and said, "No, Nicky, she wants you to pray for her."

I swallowed the lump in my throat and took a few steps toward the little girl. As I walked I prayed silently in my heart. *Dear Jesus, I'm scared. I don't know what to do. I don't want these people to be hurt. Please help me.*

I reached out and took the little girl's knees in my hands. They were nothing but skin wrapped around frail bones—so weak and damaged. The deacon held her up in front of me as a crowd pressed around close to watch. I closed my eyes, trying to think of the right words to say. I didn't even know how to begin. I opened my mouth to pray, but the only word I got out was "Jesus."

At that second I felt a strange sensation running through my hands and body. I could literally feel the joints and muscles inside the little girl's knees begin to move and strengthen. I could hear her bones beginning to crack and shift, and her legs growing tighter and starting to swell. I felt it and I saw it. The girl began to cry out, "Mama! Mama!"

I was so startled I had to take my hands away. I'd never experienced anything so undeniably miraculous.

The deacon and the mother took the girl by the hands and helped her as she took a few steps toward me. She continued to cry as she slowly began to shift more weight onto her feet. Her steps became more sure and deliberate. Suddenly she was walking on her own, her eyes wide and beaming, shocked at what had just happened to her. No one could believe their eyes, including me.

I was so shaken by the experience that I left before the service was finished. People were still praying at the front of the church, and I was expected to continue ministering to people coming forward, but I could no longer stay. I didn't even wait to collect my check for speaking, but simply left the building and started driving away in my car. It was the most powerful event I had ever experienced in God's presence.

I knew this little girl's healing had nothing to do with me. It was her mother's amazing and persistent faith that made her whole. I'm sure the mother was convinced that my prayers somehow unleashed the power and authority of the Holy Spirit, but the fact is, it was her belief in God's power that strengthened her daughter's legs.

Since that time I've seen God heal numerous people in my presence. Sometimes he works through me, and other times through those around me. But still I've always known that my ministry was not one of healing. I was called to preach salvation and lead people to Jesus, and I've never allowed myself to waiver from that calling. God may take my ministry on detours from time to time, but still he expects me to remain true to my calling within his earthly kingdom.

AN OPEN, PRAYERFUL HEART

To be able to follow the Spirit and be sensitive to all his detours, we must first have an open, prayerful heart that stays connected with God. Jesus is our greatest example of this.

No aspect of Jesus' life shines more brightly than his dependence on prayer and communion with his heavenly Father. It's the defining characteristic of his ministry, the strength behind all he said and did. Jesus prayed constantly, at every opportunity. He prayed for sinners, for his disciples, for wisdom and guidance, for his food and water, for everything. And he often went away to be alone so he could listen for the Spirit's voice without distraction. Prayer is the portal by which the Holy Spirit is allowed access into our hearts and minds, and any serious inquiry into God's guidance and direction must begin with this simple act of communication.

When we pray, we can be completely honest. Jesus knows our hearts, our motives, our thoughts, our sins and struggles. He understands our pain and temptation, because he felt it himself: "For we do not have a high priest who is unable to sympathize with our weaknesses, but we have one who has been tempted in every way, just as we are—yet was without sin. Let us then approach the throne of grace with confidence, so that we may receive mercy and find grace to help us in our time of need" (Hebrews 4:15-16).

Jesus isn't surprised by our struggles; what's surprising is only that we're so seldom willing to let him help us through them. He understands us much better than we understand ourselves. He made us. He lived among us. He knows what we're going through. And part of being an effective tool for Christ is being willing to open up our hearts and souls to him—to allow him to share with us in our successes and our failures.

After forty years in God's service I've learned that the only way I can effectively minister to others is to first allow God to minister to me. I can only give out what God has poured into my heart. When I speak, I put every ounce of myself into reaching others with God's message. I'm usually one of the first to arrive and the last to leave at my outreach crusades. I can't make myself go home until I know that every person has been prayed for and embraced with God's goodness. I literally empty myself on behalf of the lost until I have nothing left to give.

By the time November arrives each year, I'm completely spent—physically, spiritually, and emotionally. So I take the last two months of the year to allow God to revive me. Like Jesus, I go to the mountaintop to pray—not literally but spiritually. For two months each year I focus my energies on getting refilled by God's Spirit—on prayer, study, and meditation. I lay everything at the feet of Jesus—my sins, my failures, my concerns, my questions. I tell Jesus of the things I'm sorry for and the things I'm proud of. I lay out my plans for the coming year and ask for his direction. Then I wait for a response. I spend hours in his presence, waiting, watching, listening for his still, small voice in my spirit.

During these times of seclusion God has never failed to come through for me, to impart his will and vision into my heart, to speak to my soul. He either gives the plans I've laid out his blessing, or he redirects my thoughts and sends me down another path. My prayers have never gone unanswered. And by the time each new year arrives, my spirit is full and revived, ready once more to be emptied on behalf of the lost and hopeless.

ENCOURAGEMENT FOR PASTORS

That's one of the reasons I have such a burden and love in my heart for pastors. So many times pastors go year after year ministering to a congregation, trying their best to stay in God's will, to lead and shepherd their church in the Lord. It's often a thankless and difficult job with little pay and a lot of responsibility. They're expected to be flawless in the pulpit, always upbeat, never depressed, constantly ready for any crisis. So much of their time is spent ministering to others that they seldom have time to get refilled by the Lord. And many times they work tirelessly to keep their people happy, only to see family after family leave their fellowship to join the exciting megachurch down the street.

I often encourage congregations to give their pastors regular times away from the church to simply rest and pray. These times of sabbatical are crucial to their effectiveness in leading and shepherding the body. Satan's greatest weapon against one of God's evangelists or pastors is discouragement and spiritual fatigue, and the only way to combat these feelings is through a deep communion with the Father—through a regular time of prayer and replenishment by God's Spirit.

When churches encourage their pastors to do this, they almost always find that they come back excited and revived, filled with new ideas and a fresh sense of compassion and vision. They're ready to take their churches to the next level.

We all get tired and discouraged, and God is there to help when we do. More than anything on earth, God needs followers who understand the importance of going to him in prayer and meditation, preparing their hearts for greater sensitivity to the Holy Spirit.

A Torch for Battle

As the guiding light for our lives, the Holy Spirit's fire is also a war torch for our every spiritual battle. It is a fire that consumes evil. We are to obediently follow the Spirit's lead in warfare without doubting his ways.

PUSHING US FORWARD INTO BATTLE

Just weeks ago in Fort Smith, Arkansas, I was visiting over lunch with Don Hutchings, the senior pastor of a church there. He told me of a study he's been doing on the concept of the Holy Spirit as comforter. Scripture often refers to the Spirit in this manner, and we usually assume it means that he helps us through our grief or reassures us when we're down. But Don explained that the English word *comfort* was a word also used centuries ago by English kings to inspire their military, driving them toward the front lines. It's a term of war that includes the meaning of "to push toward battle."

In one of King David's most quoted yet misunderstood psalms, he says, "Even though I walk through the valley of the shadow of death, I will fear no evil, for you are with me; your rod and your staff, they *comfort* me" (Psalm 23:4). I think David wasn't asking God to remove this evil; he was asking to be pushed toward battle, to be forced to face the enemy head-on. He was ready to go to war with Satan, not hide from him!

When the apostle Paul was inspiring his brothers in the faith to remember their purpose as Christians and their reward in heaven, he told them to "comfort one another with these words" (1 Thessalonians 4:18, KJV). In effect he was saying, "Push each other forward in our battle against the evil one."

And when Jesus promised his disciples that the Comforter would be coming after his death, it was an announcement of war. The Holy Spirit would both inspire and empower them toward front-line spiritual warfare. This is a dimension of God's Spirit that's very real yet too seldom understood and embraced.

If you want to see God's Spirit at work in full glory on earth, take a trip to the front lines of battle where the war between good and evil—the battle for human souls—is being fought with intensity. If you want to feel Satan's wrath, just spend some time on his turf talking to the people he keeps in bondage and telling them about Jesus. Watch him raise his ugly head to try to intimidate and mock you.

Nothing makes Satan angrier or more nervous than when one of God's people carries the flashlight of grace into the damp darkness of his dungeon. That's when he fights the hardest. And that's when we see the Holy Spirit shine most mightily.

OPENING CONFLICT

When you're fighting for someone's soul, the true battle is in the spiritual realm. Before you can reach a person for Christ, you have to first wage war on those deceptive spirits that keep that person in bondage—those sinful habits and demons that hold him or her back from accepting Jesus' love and forgiveness.

When our ministry team brings several vanloads of people into a gang-infested inner-city area, our first priority is to take spiritual control from Satan and his demons. We wage war through the power of prayer and intercession, asking God's Spirit to take dominion over the people and the region we're trying to reach.

Sometimes the victory is immediate. Within minutes we're moving through the streets with ease, ministering with might as the Spirit rains conviction on the wounded and hurting souls of the neighborhood. In such moments I've seen many dozens of people on their knees before God, pleading for repentance and salvation. When God's Spirit moves, there's no end to the possibilities before us.

At other times this spiritual battle is not so easy. Satan's hold is stronger and the demons fiercer. The harder we pray, the angrier and more defiant these evil warriors become, and the battle for spiritual control wages on longer and harder than anyone had expected. With God's help we persevere, however, and his Spirit never loses.

SENSING SOMETHING WRONG

Just a few months ago, during one of our many hit-and-run outreaches in Houston, we sensed that a spirit of violence and anger surrounded us. Satan was determined not to lose his grip on the neighborhoods we had entered.

Late one evening we unloaded our speakers and lights on a vacant corner of a government housing project. We set up in the back corner of the gated complex while volunteers scoured the area, going door to door, inviting residents to come hear a free music concert on their block. They wore orange and green T-shirts with the word TRUCE emblazoned across the front, identifying them as our workers. A handful of prayer warriors began walking around the area, interceding on our behalf, praying a hedge of protection around our volunteers and the neighborhood. Before long, about three hundred people began flocking to the area, curious to see what was happening. After several hundred people had gathered, Patrick, my son-in-law, thanked them for coming and introduced a group of young Christian rap artists.

I stood to one side, watching and praying as the events unfolded. The music blared and the singers bounced in unison, witnessing to the crowd through the lyrics of their songs. People were enjoying the concert, moving with the music, laughing at all the right times. And volunteers continued to walk and pray around the area. On the surface it seemed as if all was going well. But in my spirit I sensed something different. Something was wrong. Somehow I knew Satan wouldn't give up without a fight.

To one side, a handful of young, hardened gang members were standing and watching on the corner, mumbling among themselves. From time to time I noticed them giving hand signals to other members of their gang in a different part of the neighborhood, asserting their authority. They weren't happy about this strange group intruding onto their turf.

Several drunks and addicts wandered into the crowd and began dancing and disrupting the performance. One older man, drunk and disorderly, walked up to the front and took the microphone from one of the young rappers.

"Hey, you kids," he said, slurring loudly into the mike, "you listen to my brothers sing. These guys are good singers and you need to pay attention." He was staggering back and forth, pointing to the crowd as he spoke. Patrick quickly walked toward him and took the microphone out of his hand. The man became angry, cursing loudly and screaming obscenities. Several volunteers escorted him away from the front of the crowd.

I could tell we were under spiritual attack, so I stepped up my intercessory pleas. *Father, bring these evil spirits into submission. Send your angels to take control of this area. Give us authority over the evil that binds this neighborhood.*

"YOU'RE IN THE WRONG NEIGHBORHOOD"

Across the street a young woman began dancing. She was dressed in extremely tight shorts and a midriff top. As she gyrated seductively to the music, oblivious to the Christian lyrics, she drew the attention of the crowd. Several men began to jeer and chant.

Dear God, I prayed, *why can't we get control over this concert? Please help us!*

My daughter Alicia walked over to the woman and placed her hand on her shoulder. "Excuse me, ma'am," she said. "You're a wonderful dancer, but you're really distracting the people from our concert."

The woman looked at her indignantly and continued dancing. Alicia persisted.

"I really hate to bother you, but you're interrupting what we're trying to do here, and it would help us a lot if you could stop for just a while."

The woman stopped dancing, crossed her arms, and walked angrily over to the side of the street. There she stood, glaring at Alicia and the singers, arms still folded tightly across her chest.

I turned to see a young gang member walking in my direction. His baggy shirt hung down to his knees, and his pant legs dragged on the ground behind him. As he came closer, I extended my hand in his direction.

"My name is Nicky Cruz," I said.

His eyes were cold and empty. He took my hand and pulled me forward, trying to make me fall down. "You're in the wrong neighborhood," he said, anger permeating his voice.

"No, I'm not," I told him. "I'm here to tell you that Jesus loves you, and you need to show some respect."

The boy jerked his hand away as he turned his back to me. He glared at me over his shoulder while he moved back toward his friends.

Just then another woman came walking toward us from across the street. She was a middle-aged woman with fire in her eyes. "What are you people doing here?" she screamed at the top of her lungs, still moving in our direction. "Get off this corner! This is my corner!" Her voice carried above the music.

She stopped in front of the curb, just a few feet from the crowd, and stood with her hands firmly on her hips. "I don't know who you people think you are, or what you think you're doing, but you better get off my corner!"

She cursed and swore at the crowd, drawing attention away from the frustrated entertainers. They continued to sing, trying to maintain control over the audience. A couple of TRUCE volunteers tried to calm the woman, but she pulled away and began swearing at them. Eventually, she just stood to one side and watched in defiance and rage.

I found myself getting angry. Didn't God realize what was happening? *Dear God,* I prayed earnestly, *why won't you take control of this situation? Why are you letting this happen? We're trying to reach these people, but unless you help we're just wasting our time. We need you to intervene, God! Help us, please!*

It was one of the most frustrating street crusades I could remember. No matter how hard we tried, the enemy seemed to get the upper hand, thwarting our efforts at every turn.

A DIFFERENT VOICE

As the music died down, Patrick took the microphone and began to witness to the crowd. "You hear a lot of voices in your neighborhood," he began. "Those voices tell you that no one cares, that life is hopeless, that the answer to your problems is found in drugs and alcohol. Those voices tell you that if you want to be somebody, you do it through joining a street gang; that respect is found only through fear.

"But tonight you're hearing a different voice. We're here tonight to tell you that there's hope, that there's a way out; that you don't have to live a life of fear and anger and hopelessness. Jesus died on a cross so you would no longer have to live in darkness and hatred.

"We're here to tell you that Jesus loves you, no matter what you've done or who you've done it with. He wants to come into your life and make you a new person, to set you free—free from this life of bitterness and hatred and spiritual poverty. Let Jesus love you and set you free!"

As Patrick continued to speak, I noticed Alicia move over beside the young girl who had been dancing in front of the crowd. "I hope you're not upset with me," she told her. "I didn't mean to embarrass you in front of your friends."

The young girl looked at her and uncrossed her arms. "That's okay," she said. "I didn't know this was church music, or I wouldn't have danced like that. I hope you're not upset with me."

"Of course not," Alicia assured her. They continued to talk as Patrick encouraged people to come forward and accept Christ.

Laura, one of our staff members, walked over behind the middle-aged woman who had been cursing at the musicians. She was still standing in anger with her arms folded tightly. Laura stood behind her and began to pray, pleading with God to soften her heart and release her wrath.

One by one, people began walking toward the front. Everywhere I looked people were weeping in repentance. First a few came, followed by a handful more, and soon a flood of people came forward, each wanting prayer and forgiveness. Patrick opened his arms wide and began to pray as the people moved toward him. God was beginning to move among us.

At that moment, I noticed two small boys about seven years old standing beneath one of the amplifiers. I recognized one as Jeremy, the seven-year-old son of one of our TRUCE volunteers, and the other was a child from a nearby apartment complex. Jeremy was standing beside him, talking, gesturing with his hands as he spoke.

The boy listened intently as Jeremy spoke, looking directly into his eyes the entire time. Suddenly I understood that Jeremy was witnessing to his new friend. Though I wasn't near, I could imagine what he was saying through his gesturing—about Jesus, how he came to earth in the form of a man to live among us, how he died on a cross to pay for our sins, and how through his blood we can now be set free from the sin that binds us. For several minutes I watched as he explained the gospel in great detail.

Then Jeremy reached out and put his hand on the young boy's shoulder. He leaned in close and looked the young boy in the eye. I could tell what he was saying: "Would you like to ask Jesus to forgive you of your sins and receive him as your Savior?"

The boy nodded, then they both bowed their heads as Jeremy began to pray, his hand still on the boy's shoulder. I fought back tears as I watched the two of them bowing before God and the world, deep in communion with their Savior, sharing a moment so precious and gentle. Seldom have I witnessed a more touching display of God's great love and grace.

When he finished praying, Jeremy looked the boy in the eye and said something to him. They both smiled and hugged. I could no longer contain my tears.

Jeremy took him by the hand and led him over to a quiet place beside our van on the street. There the boys sat on the curb as Jeremy began filling out a small green response card—the one used by our ministry to contact and track new Christians from our crusades. The boy spelled out each letter of his name as Jeremy carefully filled out every line of the card.

"LET THE TEARS FLOW"

As I stood watching this tender scene, God began speaking to me in my spirit, convicting me of the wrongful anger that had been rising in me earlier. *Nicky,* he said, *don't ever think that I don't know what I'm doing. I know Satan's tricks, but I always get the last word. Don't ever question my methods.*

Dear God, I prayed, *please forgive me for doubting you. I know you're in control, even when it seems that you're not. You always have been. I'll never question you again.*

I looked back at the crowd just in time to see the angry middle-aged woman making her way toward the front. She was wiping away tears from her eyes. Laura placed her hand on the woman's shoulders and together they began to pray.

Several of the young gang members started walking toward Patrick, heads bowed. Some TRUCE volunteers saw them and walked over in their direction. For several minutes they stood witnessing to the boys. Two of them fell to their knees in repentance as a TRUCE worker laid hands on them and prayed on their behalf. The rest of their gang stood and watched from a distance. A few of them left in anger.

Then I noticed Alicia ministering to the young woman who had been dancing earlier. Her heavy, dark makeup was running down the sides of her face as she wept.

"Have you ever asked Jesus to forgive you of your sins?" Alicia asked her.

"No, I haven't," said the girl. "I'm not even sure if God wants to forgive me."

Alicia smiled and began sharing the gospel with the young woman. She listened intently to every word. She never stopped crying.

"Would you like me to pray for you?" Alicia asked.

"Yes, I would," the girl answered.

Alicia placed her hand on the woman's shoulders and began praying for her. Tears poured down her cheeks as she fumbled to find a tissue. Alicia could tell she was embarrassed, so she offered her a corner of her shirt. The girl put her entire face into Alicia's shirt, smearing makeup and tears all over the front. I almost had to laugh.

"I don't know why I'm crying," the woman said. "I'm happy, but I can't seem to stop. What's wrong with me?"

Alicia smiled. "That's the Holy Spirit. God is ministering to your soul through his Spirit. Don't try to stop it. Just let the tears flow."

Together they stood and wept, finally laughing with joy over the girl's newfound faith in God.

Once again I felt a conviction in my spirit. In spite of my doubts, in spite of how it had seemed earlier, God was doing a mighty work in the hearts of this broken neighborhood. What seemed at first to be a failed attempt on our part turned into one of our most moving and fruitful street crusades.

Precious Jesus, I prayed. *Thank you for your goodness and your mercy. Thank you for once again raining your power in our midst. We give you all the glory and authority. Jesus, thank you for your Holy Spirit and for loosing your might among us. We love you, Jesus.*

The spirit's creative Blaze

Music and drama have always been big parts of what we do, and through the years we've experimented with a number of different creative methods of fashioning and presenting God's message of hope. If we think it might help bring people to the feet of Jesus, we're willing to try it. We've seen the Spirit truly at work through these artistic endeavors.

GANGSTER MUSIC

I remember a period several years ago, while we were still experimenting with our hit-and-run outreaches, trying to figure out how to best reach people in the inner city. We had tried a number of different approaches and were constantly changing the format and the type of music we used in an effort to attract the greatest number of people. It was apparent that most inner-city kids listened to hip-hop and rap. Personally I don't care much for this type of music, and neither did most of the people we worked with, so we were reluctant to try it. It also seemed impossible to find any young Christian singers who were doing rap music. Still, we knew we needed to make an effort since so many kids in urban neighborhoods seemed to like it.

While planning a crusade in the New York area with a number of local pastors and evangelists, we brought the matter up for discussion. It was not well received. Not one person in the room thought we should pursue the idea. Rap music was seen as a form of gangster music, associated with crime and violence and anger. Our job, they believed, was to bring people to Christ so they would no longer have an interest in rap. They couldn't imagine that God would bless these efforts.

Still, we persisted. I was convinced that if we were going to reach inner-city kids, we needed to first get inside their music. So we began to pray and put out a search for some young Christian rap artists. God put us in contact with three young kids from the Bronx, who called themselves Brothers Inc. 4 Da Lord. We didn't know anything about them, but they offered to help us, so we trusted God and agreed.

The first time we let them perform at one of our hit-and-run outreaches, we couldn't believe the response. Nor had we any idea of the anointing God had placed on these three young men and their music. They told us beforehand that they preferred to sing "free style," but we weren't sure what that meant. We found out that it was totally improvisational rapping. While music played in the background, they would take turns making up lyrics on the spot, often prophesying to the people around them through the power of the Holy Spirit.

During this particular street crusade, the group singled out some young boys in the crowd—kids who had been playing basketball before we arrived in the neighborhood—and began singing about them. Their prophetic words were hard-hitting and convicting, exposing the boys' sins and asking the question, "What are you going to do with your life?" Most amazingly, the lyrics rhymed. The singers explained to me later that the words simply come to them as they perform, placed in their minds by the Holy Spirit, a form of prophecy.

For the first time since we'd begun doing hit-and-run outreaches, people began coming forward during the music, before we even had the chance to share the gospel and make a call for repentance. The power behind the boys' music so convicted the young people of their sin that they came forward and stood at the front of the crowd, weeping in repentance. It took us off guard, but we quickly grabbed a few volunteers and went to pray with the people coming forward.

I had seen God's Spirit work in many ways, but I'd never seen him work so powerfully through music. Since that time we've begun to use rap and hip-hop music exclusively in our hit-and-run outreaches, and God continues to be glorified through it.

DIRT I CAN'T FORGET

Drama is another way we've seen God's Spirit work with blazing power in our ministry, especially through the dramatic retelling of my own story.

I often wonder why God gave me such a good memory. You'd think that a person with a past as sordid and violent and hard as mine would be blessed with the gift of forgetting. But, for some reason, God didn't see it that way. He gave me the kind of memory that can recall the smallest details of the most horrid parts of my past, even from my days as a child in Puerto Rico. These images stand out in my mind today as clearly and vividly as the day they happened. At times I've wished God would wash away these horrible memories that plague me, of all the violence and hate and anger of my past—the things I've seen and done. Yet I continue to recall them with the greatest clarity.

I know that's no accident. God keeps my memory sharp and my past fresh in my mind for a reason. Every time I get up to share my testimony, to tell of the pain of my previous life and the hopelessness that God saved me from, people respond. The Holy Spirit uses my past to soften hearts and bring conviction to the spirits of unbelievers. When they see that I've been where they are, that I understand the hate and fear and spiritual poverty that defines their world, the walls come down. And God uses this opportunity to touch them, to draw them to himself.

The message I bring to the lost is a simple one: Jesus loves you, and he wants to set you free from your bondage—your hate and violence and fear—no matter what you've done or how horrible your past is. This message gets through because it's the one that people steeped in sin most need to hear. I stand before them as a living testament to God's unbelievable grace and mercy. They know that if God can take a person like me, a hardened, cold-blooded kid from the streets, and completely change my heart and future, then maybe he'll do the same for them. Through my testimony, God is able to touch the hearts of some of the coldest, most unreachable people on earth—the ones who are so despised, so hated, that they can't imagine being loved by anyone, much less the Creator of the universe.

That's why God helps me remember.

Early in my ministry God laid on my heart the importance of telling my story. He's shown me time and again how effective a simple testimony can be in stirring hearts toward repentance and bringing people to Jesus. While so many preachers and evangelists spend their time trying to convince people to come to God through lengthy explanations of the spiritual laws, or a detailed exegesis on the inerrancy of Scripture, I simply tell the lost what they most need to hear—that Jesus loves them and wants to come in and set them free from their spiritual poverty. He wants to be their friend and father—the father they never had, the father who will love and protect them. I tell them what he has done in my life and invite them to let him do the same in theirs. The genius of this message is its simplicity, just like the gospel. And God never fails to use my story to draw people to him.

NOT YOUR EVERYDAY CHURCH PLAY

When Jesus had a message that he wanted people to remember, he usually relayed it in the form of a parable. He told stories, because that's what people relate to. It was a way of wrapping flesh and bones around a principle.

That's why I've always been a firm believer in drama. At its core, drama is nothing more than a way of taking storytelling to the highest level, using all the senses to bring a story to life, drawing people in and letting them live the story as it unfolds before them.

Our TRUCE outreach ministry today is best known for its *Run Baby Run* stage productions. It's probably the best tool we've found for reaching thousands of people with the gospel—people who would never step into a church building or sit still for a lecture on God or the Bible.

This isn't your everyday church play we're talking about. In fact, I'm often wary of inviting mainstream Christians to the show, because many come away offended by the violence and realism and street language portrayed on the stage. The production is hard-hitting and real, taking the audience into the middle of the hate and anger of life in the ghetto. Our intent is to show a true picture of the dead-end world of gangs and drugs and prostitution—the hopelessness of selling out to sin in the inner city. And that's not always an easy thing to watch.

The script is based on my life story, and the production is every bit as professional as a full-scale off-Broadway show. It takes a complete staff of stagehands and more than forty actors, dancers, and singers to produce. The core characters in the cast are portrayed by a handful of trained actors from New York City, and the rest of the cast is hired through local auditions conducted by the director. The production runs four or five nights in a row, usually in the largest stadium or auditorium available (or at least the largest we can afford), sometimes two and three shows a night. On average we'll have reached between twenty thousand and thirty thousand people by the end of the run, many of whom will have heard the gospel for the first time. (As hard as it is for most Christians to believe, we still encounter people regularly in this country who have never been told about Jesus.)

The play begins with my life as a boy in Puerto Rico, growing up in a family deeply immersed in the occult. It moves through the day that my father put me on a plane to New York City and my experiences as a homeless child on the streets, as I turned to gangs and violence for survival. It ends at the moment I finally broke down and gave my life to Jesus at the beckoning of a street preacher, David Wilkerson.

At this point in the production the house lights come on and I take to the stage with a microphone. I introduce myself then take the audience inside my mind at the moment I surrendered to Christ, how he came in and touched my heart, changing my life and future forever.

By the time I make a call for repentance, people have been so moved by the power of God's touch on my life that many are brought to their knees in conviction. It's not uncommon for us to see over a thousand people coming forward in a stadium to receive Christ. God has no trouble bringing people to repentance. The hard part for us is keeping up with their names and seeing that local churches remain true to their commitments to these new believers. Ultimately, though, we trust the Holy Spirit to continue the work within the lives of those who accept Christ as their Savior.

A SURPRISING CALL

Before the *Run Baby Run* production was developed, we used a play centered on the life of a young gang member on the streets. It chronicled the hate and futility of his life in the inner city. By the end of the play we saw him come to repentance before Christ at the feet of a street preacher. Though the story line was similar to my life, the play was a fictional piece of drama that we borrowed from another ministry. There was music in the background but no original songs or dances. And the amateur cast was rather small. Though it was well done and effective, we all felt that somehow it could be better. We continued to pray that God would show us a new and better way to evangelize and reach the lost.

One day, Patrick and Alicia were brainstorming with two dear friends, pastor Aimee Cortese and her son, Joseph Henry. Some years earlier, Aimee had founded the Crossroads Tabernacle, a small but dynamic church in the Bronx, and now Joseph was the senior pastor there. He's also an accomplished musician who's written a number of songs and once toured with Roberta Flack and a handful of other celebrities.

During the meeting, Alicia casually made the statement, almost in passing, "Wouldn't it be great if we had a play based on my dad's life?" It seemed like an intriguing idea, so they began discussing it further. Joseph showed little interest in the concept, but for some reason they persisted, especially Alicia. "I'm sure you could write it," she told Joseph. Why don't you consider it?"

He seemed surprised by her request. "Why would you ask me?" he said. "I'm a musician. I don't write drama."

"I just think you could do it," answered Alicia. "We've been praying that God would give us a vision for a new type of production, and I really think this could work. And I think you're the person who could help us with it."

For several moments he sat silently. Patrick and Alicia wondered what he was thinking.

They didn't know that Joseph had been given a prophecy just three months earlier regarding his talents. While Joseph was sitting in a morning service listening to a lesson on the subject of Gideon, the guest speaker suddenly stopped her message and walked over to where Joseph was sitting. She told him that God had given her a revelation regarding his life, and she went into great detail describing it. "God will soon call you to reach thousands upon thousands through drama," she said. "You'll be called upon to do great things through the art of theater. When that calling comes, don't turn your back on it. Trust God to help you."

Joseph was confused by this message and thought that perhaps the woman had prophesied to the wrong person. He hadn't written a play since his days in high school English class, and never had he felt that drama was his gift or calling. He dismissed her words and went on with his ministry.

He forgot about the prophecy until Patrick and Alicia showed up. He finally told them about it, and agreed to Alicia's suggestion.

"I'm not sure if I can do it," he said. "I'm not even sure where to start. But it looks like God has called me to do this, so I have to make the effort."

DRAMATIC POWER

Though we had no idea what to expect, we began praying and giving Joseph the information and support he needed. Miraculously, he seemed to know exactly what to do. He began calling on the talents of studio musicians he'd worked with in the past, and he spent the next few months writing and brainstorming. Then one day he presented us with a first draft of a musical drama, complete with music and lyrics. None of us were prepared for the quality of the production, both with regard to the music and to the dialogue. He titled the play *Run Baby Run,* after my book.

As exciting as the whole thing seemed, we never imagined taking on a production of this magnitude. We wondered seriously if we could ever do justice to the amazing script God had provided. But we trusted God and began to pray he would somehow put the pieces into place. He provided beyond our wildest dreams.

One by one, talented people came to our side. We began to see the project grow and evolve as time went by. I worked closely with Joseph to fine-tune the manuscript, and we began auditioning and hiring the cast and stagehands. Before we knew it, we were ready for our first performance.

The play premiered in an old RKO theater in the Bronx, and we knew immediately that God's anointing was all over it. Crowds began lining up at three in the afternoon, and by showtime the line stretched for eight blocks. We ended up performing multiple shows, two or three a day over the next four days, to fit everyone in. At the end of each performance, people responded in ways we never imagined. Thousands were brought under the conviction of the Holy Spirit through the play's powerful drama and music.

Today, when we think back to the story of how this drama was conceived and produced by a handful of unlikely novices, it seems almost impossible to believe.

JESUS THE SURGEON

Less than a month ago I watched this amazing production again. Through the years we've continued to hone the play, to tighten the dialogue and add new songs here and there, always working to make it a bit better and more effective.

As I view this production today, I'm more humbled than ever by what God has done in my life and by the enormity of his love and grace and goodness. I'm continually in awe of his blessing on my ministry and future. Why he would choose to work so mightily in the life of a poor kid from Puerto Rico, a gangster from the ghetto, a simple man who still struggles to speak good English, remains forever a mystery to me. I am blessed far beyond reason.

In my heart I still see myself as a helpless and needy nineteen-year-old boy, kneeling before the altar, weeping in repentance and asking God to come into my heart and be my Savior. Like a baby longing for his mother's milk, I drank deeply of God's love and forgiveness. I could almost feel his gentle arms wrapping themselves around my cold body, comforting, warming, snuggling. For the first time in my life I felt loved. He became my Father, and I became his son. I literally felt the warmth of the Holy Spirit come into my soul and embrace my heart. It was as real as any experience I've ever had.

When I speak I often search my vocabulary for ways to express this supernatural sensation, the moment when Jesus stepped in and changed my life, but I've yet to find a way to do it justice. The best way I've found is through a simple analogy.

I tell people that I felt as if I were on an operating table, cold and angry and confused, and Jesus was the surgeon standing over me. My heart was broken. He gently reached over and closed my eyes, then he opened up my chest and reached deep inside of me and pulled my heart out. He held it in his hands, a heart filled with the hatred and anger and bitterness that consumed me—the brokenness of my past and the curse that was destroying my life and soul. Then Jesus slowly took my heart, brought it to his lips, and kissed it. He caressed it and mended the wounds. Then he placed it back in my chest and closed me up. I knew in an instant that I was better, that my heart was no longer broken. At that moment I knew I was a new creation. I had a new heart—a heart of love and compassion and repentance. All the feelings of hate and resentment were gone. My sins were forgiven. At long last I was free!

I still fight back tears every time I use this analogy. The moment Jesus came into my heart and saved me is the most cherished experience of my life. Before that time no one had ever kissed my heart. It was what I needed most from my new Father.

Thank you, precious Jesus!

STILL THAT LITTLE BOY

Today I am still that little boy, and he is still my Father. Everywhere I go I look to him to walk beside me, hold my hand, lead me. When I stumble and fall, he reaches down and picks me up. He dusts off my clothes, kisses the hurt, then continues with me down the road.

When I do something right, I see him smiling, clapping, showing his support. When I do something wrong, he scolds and disciplines. When I get tired and weary, he holds me up, beckoning me forward and encouraging me not to give up. When I'm frightened, he takes my hand. When I'm sad, he kisses my heart once more.

I look to Jesus for help and guidance in everything I do, and he has never failed me. He has always been there when I needed him.

This loving relationship I have with my Father is one that began more than forty years ago. It hasn't always been easy. At times I've pulled away from him, tried to go my own way, even rebelled, but he has always been there to receive me with his arms outstretched, waiting for me to turn back to him. His faithfulness has never waned—he's the perfect friend and Father. My faithfulness to him, however, was a quality I had to learn, one that I'm still working on every day. It's a lifelong process.

When I first gave my heart to Jesus, I had no idea where this newfound faith would take me. I was scared and alone, wondering how he would rescue me from the people and things of my past, the gangs and drugs that held me captive. I didn't know how to be his child. But he showed me, mentored me along the way.

My life and ministry today have been shaped entirely by the things God taught me through those early years as a young follower of Christ. I was being fashioned and groomed into an evangelist, a minister of God's grace. He was teaching me to trust him, to rely on his strength and authority, not my own. And he was showing me the full extent of his power over evil.

Throughout those years I witnessed firsthand what can happen when we allow God's Spirit to be loosed within and among us, when we tap into his glory, when we step out of the way and allow him to work and move and minister through us. I learned the power of prayer and the importance of laying worries and decisions at the feet of Jesus. I learned what it means to walk in the Spirit, by the light of his holy fire.

power and a passion for souls

We're never closer to the heart and pulse of God than when we're reaching out to the lost. That's a truth I wish I could impart into the soul of every pastor and believer on earth. If you want to see God up close and personal, to feel his smile shining down upon you, to sense his tender nod of acknowledgment— just reach out and take a sinner by the hand and lead him to his Savior. There's no greater joy this side of heaven than embracing a new babe in Christ, kissing a newly redeemed soul on the cheek, knowing that you had a hand in introducing him or her to Jesus.

I truly believe that most followers of Christ want to win souls and are held back only because they feel unequipped. A number of churches are not doing a good job in teaching their members how to witness to a friend or family member, and some pastors aren't doing enough to lay this burden on the hearts of their congregation.

Too often we make evangelism much more frightening and complicated than it needs to be. We're afraid of making mistakes, of saying too much too soon, of turning people away from God instead of bringing them closer. Believe me, I understand those fears. In fact, I've made about every mistake imaginable while sharing the gospel, but God has always worked through them.

I'm not saying that ministering to people is easy. Like any task it requires commitment and sacrifice. Sometimes it takes guts, especially when you try to reach people who are hardened and cold. I've been persecuted for my beliefs, spat on, laughed at, shot at, even knifed a few times—and perhaps you will be too. Satan doesn't let go of his slaves without a fight, and he never fights fairly.

But the rewards are endless and far outweigh any amount of displeasure or persecution you will feel.

DESPERATE DESIRE

In Genesis we read the story of Jacob's wife, Rachel, and her desperate desire to have a child. She could no longer bear the thought of living without knowing the joy of childbirth, without experiencing all that was intended for her as a woman. In Jewish culture a woman without a child was looked on with disdain, as an incomplete person, a body with no purpose. Rachel's pain was unbearable, and she cried out to Jacob, "Give me children, or I'll die!" (30:1).

Bringing a soul to Christ is very much like giving birth. The Holy Spirit conceives the desire in our hearts, and we then begin to nurture the process, growing in our relationship, praying for them regularly. We feel the time coming near and long to see our new baby delivered. We want to hold and nurture our new child, to experience both the pain and joy of childbirth. When it finally happens, when our new baby is born, we don't want to ever put it down. We play and cuddle and mentor God's new creation. We plant and water, praying that God will give the increase. All we can think about is helping our child grow and flourish and take on the image of Christ.

If only every follower of Christ felt this same sense of passion and urgency to bring a new child into God's kingdom! What if we each decided that we could no longer live with the thought of being barren? What if the desire burned within our hearts until we could no longer contain it, until we finally kept crying out to God, "Give me a spiritual child, or I will die!"?

You and I both know what would happen: God would honor those prayers. And the world would never be the same. With God's help we could turn the world upside down (or rather, right-side up).

But everywhere I go I meet Christians who have never felt the joy of leading a soul to Christ. They come to me asking for advice, usually with heads bowed and eyes cast downward, embarrassed by the awkwardness of this confession. I tell them not to be ashamed by this fact but instead excited that the Holy Spirit is convicting their hearts.

"The first step in sharing your faith is developing a burning desire to do so," I tell them. And we can count on the Holy Spirit to ignite this desperate desire within us, if we ask and allow him to. For this is exactly what the Spirit wants to do.

THE SPIRIT'S PRIMARY PURPOSE

The primary purpose of the Holy Spirit is to empower God's people to reach the lost and draw people to the Cross. Just as he convicts us of our sins, he also moves in the hearts of unbelievers, bringing them face to face with their iniquities and failures, with the futility of their lives apart from God.

When Jesus was preparing his disciples for his departure from earth, he told them, "When the Counselor comes, whom I will send to you from the Father, the Spirit of truth who goes out from the Father, *he will testify about me*. And you also must testify, for you have been with me from the beginning" (John 15:26-27).

Jesus tells us that we know the truth of the gospel because God's Spirit has revealed it to us through his words. The Holy Spirit has testified to God's grace and goodness. Our confidence in our position in God's kingdom comes not from our own hope and imagination, but from the Creator himself, from his gentle whisper in our soul. It's how we know that God's love is real and defini-tive and unwavering.

Jesus went on to explain the Holy Spirit's role like this: "When he comes, *he will convict the world of guilt* in regard to sin and righteousness and judg-ment: in regard to sin, because men do not believe in me" (John 16:8-9).

It isn't our job to convict people of their sin. The Holy Spirit is already doing that. Our role is to simply be there for them, to tell them of God's for-giveness, to share what he has done in our own lives, to tell them what the Spirit has already told us. We're not here to judge people for their sins, but to simply tell them about Jesus, to embrace them in their pain and suffering, and to love them into God's wonderful kingdom. Jesus came not to condemn the world, but to save it (John 3:17). Shouldn't we have the same attitude?

The most powerful prayer a believer can lift up to God is, "Jesus, help me to sense when I meet someone who needs your love and forgiveness. Guide me to a person who is hurting and feeling the conviction of the Holy Spirit. Then put your words on my tongue and your wisdom in my heart. Use me to draw that person to you." Once he does, we should try to reach that person through a message of comfort and encouragement. That's why it's called the "good news."

God has never failed to use a follower who's sincere and open to evange-lizing someone to Christ. That is his plan and desire for all believers.

But the majority of Christians today have never led anyone to Jesus, and many have never even tried. Either they're embarrassed by their faith, afraid they might say the wrong thing, or they simply don't know how. Whatever the rea-son, they go through life keeping their faith to themselves, living and working with unbelievers, terrified at the thought of someone asking them about Jesus.

This situation burdens my heart and spirit. I hurt for Christians who have never experienced the satisfaction of bringing a new child into the kingdom, of laying a broken heart at the feet of Jesus and witnessing his gentle touch and healing. They have no idea what they're missing. It's the single greatest experi-ence a Christian can have.

"One Great Overwhelming Factor"

The church today has somehow lost its zeal and desire to release God's power and Spirit on the world. Somewhere along the way we've convinced ourselves that God is content with our devotion, our worship, our acceptance of his grace, our commitment to pray daily and remain faithful in our service to the church. But what we lack, what we've lost, is our passion for him and his power in reaching the lost. Where is our belief that he's truly "able to do immeasurably more than all we ask or imagine, according to his power that is at work within us" (Ephesians 3:20)?

While the church of the first century grew greater in numbers with each passing day, we've stood by and watched as the church in America has declined rapidly over the past fifty years. The early church began with only a handful of believers who were filled with the Spirit and preached in the streets to a pagan world. Our churches' memberships number in the millions nationwide, yet we struggle even to pass our faith on to our children. Any honest evaluation of today's church brings us to the conclusion that we're in trouble, that our effectiveness in reaching the lost has been severely diminished.

How seldom we stop to think about what could be accomplished for the cause of Christ if believers everywhere had a unified passion and desire to save the world for Jesus.

I once heard a preacher read a letter written by an eighteen-year-old boy from Russia. He was a member of the Communist Party during the Cold War years. In it, he explains his love and devotion to the party. It's a sad letter to read because it shows just how easily a young heart can be manipulated and misguided. Yet the passion he exudes is something that every follower of Christ should long for:

> We communists have a high casualty rate. We are the ones that get
> shot, hung, ridiculed, fired from our jobs, and made as uncomfortable
> as possible. We live in virtual poverty. We keep track of every cent we

make, and we spend only what is absolutely necessary to keep ourselves alive. We have been described as fanatics. We are fanatic! Our lives are dominated by one great overwhelming factor—the struggle of world communism. It is my life, it is my people, my religion, my habit, my sweetheart, my wife, my mistress, my bread, and my meat. I work for it in the daytime; I dream of it at night. I cannot carry out a friendship, a love affair, or even a conversation without relating to the force that both guides and drives my life.

This is the kind of passion and purpose that drove the communist ideology from a small band of a few thousand followers of Lenin in the early twentieth century to eventual control over a third of the world's population. People didn't simply believe in this misguided philosophy—they completely gave themselves over to it. Lenin once said, "Give me a handful of dedicated people and I will take the world." He very nearly accomplished that goal.

I often wonder what has kept the body of Christ from developing that same kind of passion and purpose for our cause. Why don't we have the same zeal for our cause as the communists had for theirs?

Is our faith simply not that deep and consuming?

MISSING INGREDIENT

Not too long ago I heard a message given by a visiting evangelist. He had an amazing stage presence, and his words rolled off his tongue with ease and eloquence. He carried a Bible in one hand and a handkerchief in the other, and as he paced the stage, he regularly stopped to dab the sweat off his forehead. Then he would face the audience, careful to make eye contact with a few, and boom out his next sentence. It was a practiced technique that almost always got a response.

I found myself in awe of his ability to work a room, the psychology he used to keep our attention. He was a gifted communicator; no one could argue that. When he finished, we all went away thoroughly entertained.

But something was missing, something intangible, subtle, but very real. It took me awhile to put my finger on it, but I finally did.

What he lacked was passion! He had talent and knowledge, that was apparent, but his words didn't seem to come from the heart. When it was over we knew a lot about what he thought and about the breadth of his vocabulary, but not about what he felt, what his faith meant to him, about his pain and struggles, his internal battles. *Don't tell me what you think about God,* I thought, *tell me what God has done in your life, about what he is doing, about what he saved you from! Tell me what he means to you! Let me see inside your heart, not your head!*

I'm not trying to be overly critical. I know we all have different personalities, and some ministers are more emotional than others. And I'm aware that every speaker has a different approach, a different method of reaching an audience.

Yet somewhere, deep in my heart, I wonder how anyone can approach a lesson about our Lord as an exercise in communication. When it comes to Jesus, to our precious Savior, the one who loved us enough to hang on a cross, sin-free and innocent, to die so that you and I could live—when it comes to this man, how can we even mention his name without feeling passion? How is it possible to discuss his touch on our lives, to talk about the enormity of his love and grace, without sensing a flood of emotion stirring within our hearts and souls?

You can't stand before the cross detached and unaffected. You can't finger the nails without feeling the pain. You can't look into the eyes of pure love and forgiveness and discuss it as you would the weather. Jesus isn't that kind of Savior. The very nature of his life and death and resurrection, the reason for his coming, the beauty of the gospel cries out for complete and uncompromising passion!

Otherwise we've missed his message entirely.

When we truly come to understand the magnitude of what Jesus has done for us, we're no longer able to keep silent. We want to tell everyone we meet. We can't sit still while others are lost, steeped in sin and guilt and hopelessness. A passionate faith doesn't allow room for complacency.

TOO MUCH EMOTION?

People have said that, when I speak, I appeal too much to emotions. They say I tell sad stories from the street because I know it will get a response; that I implore the heart, not the head. To this charge I gladly plead guilty!

I'm a passionate person and have always worn my emotions on my sleeve. Maybe it's the Puerto Rican blood in me, but when I talk about Jesus, I get excited and I want everyone else to catch that enthusiasm. I've definitely never been one of the frozen chosen. I love my Lord with a passion, with all my heart, soul, strength…and yes, my mind. But mostly with my heart!

I speak to the heart because that's how God speaks most clearly to me. I use painful stories from the street to break people down and convict their spirits, because it's through those experiences that God's compassion for the lost has been burned into my heart and soul.

God saved me by appealing to my heart. As my faith and devotion to him grew, he began to impart knowledge and insight, an understanding of his ways, a desire to study and learn and grow even deeper in his wisdom. It's a process of mentoring and maturing, one that will continue until the day I die, but it began with an appeal to my emotions, not my intellect.

I grew up in a family that knew nothing about Jesus. My mother and father were children of the darkness, immersed in a lifestyle of the occult, blinded to the light of Jesus' wonderful grace. I remember vividly my mother's eyes. They were cold and dark and empty. Emotionless eyes. There was nothing there: no love, no feeling, no compassion…nothing but blackness. It was like staring into the pit of hell. At times I felt as if Satan himself was staring back at me through the barren, vacant eyes of my mother.

By the grace of God I was later able to lead my mother and father to the Lord. She became a powerful witness to God's wonderful forgiveness, and for the first time I was able to look into her eyes and see the love and compassion that I had always longed for. The emptiness was gone, and in its place was pure beauty, a soul free from hate and despair. She was a child of freedom.

How can we ever again be silent when we've witnessed the miraculous transformation of a soul set free from Satan's evil grip? Once we've seen what Jesus can do in and through a life devoted to his will, we become forever changed. We begin longing for all the wisdom and empowerment that the Holy Spirit offers. We can't stop ourselves from pleading on behalf of the lost, yearning to reach them with God's message.

CHAPTER NINE

Everywhere–people Needing Jesus

So many people have said to me through the years, "I don't know how you continue to sacrifice so much for the poor and helpless people of this country. What would they do without you?"

I smile and thank them, but what I'm thinking to myself is, *What would I do without them?*

I'm not sure where I would be if I didn't have people to minister to, to hurt for, to cry with, to hold in the name of Jesus. What joy would there be in my life if I could no longer clutch an abused young girl's head against my chest as I weep and pray with her? What purpose would my life serve if I could no longer embrace the pain of a streetwise, drugged-out young teenager as he comes to grips with his sin and falls at the feet of Jesus in repentance? Where would I find my passion?

This is how the Lord uses me, how he fills me with his strength and compassion, how he keeps my heart humble and my life complete. He pours his love *through* me, not just *into* me. He has instilled within me a deep and abiding love for the hopeless and weary—the rejected lepers of our day—and I am most fulfilled when I'm acting on that devotion.

NO SECRETS

I've discovered there's no mystical secret to effective evangelism. At heart I'm nothing more than a poor Latino kid from the ghetto, and God has used me to reach people from all walks of life—rock stars, doctors, lawyers, businessmen, auto mechanics, scientists, rich, poor, black, white, Asian, Spanish, tall, short, skinny. I haven't always said or done the right things while sharing with people. Like Christian, the main character in *Pilgrim's Progress,* I've often found confusion setting in, but God works through my human failures. I've never met a person I was afraid to share my faith with, and time and again, God has used me for his glory in spite of my past or limitations.

Everywhere I go I find people who need Jesus. Often they're people who spend their lives interacting with Christians, doing business with them, living next-door to them, yet no one has ever taken the time to tell them the gospel.

Awhile back I was traveling to Los Angeles on TWA for a speaking engagement. As I sat enjoying the flight, the captain of the plane came down the aisle looking for me. He'd heard I was on the plane and wanted to meet me.

After introducing himself, he said, "I just wanted to be able to tell my family I met you. My wife and kids think a lot of you, and I hear them praying for you all the time. They've read many of your books."

"That's great to hear," I told him. "Tell me about them."

He began describing his wife as a beautiful Christian woman who has raised two beautiful kids, both of whom love the Lord. But as he was speaking, I sensed a certain distance, a detached tone in his voice.

"That's wonderful," I said. "But what about you? How's your relationship with the Lord?"

He bowed his head slowly. "To be honest, I'm not a very good man. I'm an adulterer, and I'm not living like I should." He wouldn't look me in the eye as he spoke. My heart hurt for him.

"You know, Jesus can do the same for you that he has for your family," I told him. "He knows you, whether you know him or not."

Before he had a chance to respond I began witnessing to him. I told him about Jesus and the freedom he brings. I told him how he died on a cross to save us from our sins. He listened with interest, still gazing at the ground in front of me.

AIRPLANE REVIVAL

Suddenly he raised his head and looked me in the eye. "Tell me the truth," he said. "All those things you say in your books about what God has done for you…all those stories…are they really true?"

I smiled and took a step closer. "Yes, they are. You have no idea what God has done in my life. Most of the stories from my past are so brutal I've never had the heart to talk or write about them. But God didn't care. He loved me and saved me, and he can do the same for you."

Tears started running down his cheeks. He reached out, took my hand, then brought it up and held it to his forehead.

"Would you pray for me?" he said.

"Of course I will."

As I prayed for him, he sobbed like a baby there in the middle of the airplane aisle. Several of the passengers started crying along with him when they saw what was happening.

When I finished praying I could hardly contain my excitement. "The devil can't touch you anymore," I told him. "You're God's child now! Doesn't it feel wonderful?"

We spent the next five minutes talking and laughing and fellowshiping together. He couldn't stop crying the entire time. I finally told him, "You need to go fly this plane. I have to get to Los Angeles."

He went back to the cockpit, and within a few minutes the copilot came back to where I was sitting. "The captain said I should come back and talk to you," he said. I smiled, then rose from my seat and began sharing the gospel with him as well. A couple of flight attendants who were standing nearby gathered in close to listen.

We had our own little church revival right in the aisle of the airplane. When I finished, all three had received Christ as their Savior. They were crying and praying with me as the passengers sat by and watched. My head was in the clouds for the rest of the flight.

I never tire of leading people to Jesus. At heart I'm still the little kid who used to roam the streets of New York and steal food from street vendors. Only now I'm a thief for God—I shoplift souls right out from under Satan's nose. I sneak onto his turf and snatch God's precious children right out of his ugly claws.

And the best part is, he can't do anything about it!

ROBERTO

My heart still stirs when I think back to one of the first times God used me to save someone's soul. I was freshly graduated from Bible college and working as a busboy in a restaurant in California. I took the job because I needed the money, but it didn't take long to figure out that I was a pitiful employee. I'm surprised they didn't fire me after the first few days.

When I applied for the job, I thought to myself, *This is going to be a piece of cake. If I can run a gang, surely I can clean a few tables.* I soon developed a healthy respect for honest, working people. Fighting on the streets didn't do much to prepare me for a thankless job in a hot kitchen.

My first day on the job I met a fellow Puerto Rican named Roberto. He was a quiet, hard-working single man from the area, close to my age. Our foreman, however, was a Latino man who had somehow come to disdain Puerto Ricans, and tensions at the restaurant always ran at a fever pitch. He was constantly screaming and ordering us around. A few years earlier I would have laid him flat the first time he looked at me crosswise, but now, with Jesus in my life, I made the effort to hold my temper.

Several times I confronted the foreman. "You have no right to talk to us that way," I told him. "We're doing the best we can." Without fail he would stand up and dare me to back up my words. It took all the strength I could muster to walk away, especially knowing I could take him down so quickly he'd never know what happened. It was only through God's grace that I was able to turn the other cheek.

One day after my shift, I sat down to have a sandwich and bowed my head to pray. When I finished, I noticed Roberto standing over me.

"Do you always pray for your meal?" he asked me.

"Yes, I do," I answered. "God has been good to me, and I like to thank him for the food he provides."

He sat down beside me, and we made small talk for a few minutes. Then he asked, "Why don't you fight the boss? I know you're not scared. Are you just afraid of losing your job?"

"No, that's not it," I said. "I've just done enough fighting in my life, and it hasn't gotten me anywhere. Jesus has better things for me to do."

I could tell Roberto was curious about my comments, so I spent the next ten minutes sharing with him about my faith. I told him my testimony and what Jesus had done in my life. Then I invited him to accept Jesus as his Savior. "He can do the same for you, Roberto."

NOT READY

But Roberto wasn't ready to receive God's forgiveness. I knew from past conversations that he had a lot of sin in his life—sin he didn't want to give up. He wasn't yet ready to deal with his weakness for women and liquor. But that night as he lay in bed, my words weighed heavily on his heart. The next day he came to me after work to talk some more.

"I can't get what you said yesterday out of my mind," he began. "I really want to have the kind of peace in my heart that you have, but I just don't know how. I feel restless and lonely."

I took him to a booth in the back and sat down beside him.

"Roberto, just open your heart to Jesus. You can't hide anything from God. He knows about your sin. He knows what's in your heart. He knows what you're going through. Jesus wants to come in and forgive you and make you a new person, with a new life ahead of you. Why won't you open up and let him?"

He sat for a long time weighing my words. I knew he was struggling with his decision, and I gave him time to think. I simply prayed in my heart that he would accept Jesus.

Finally, he looked up and said, "Nicky, pray for me!"

"Are you sure you know what this means?" I asked him. "This is an important decision—the most important one you'll ever make. Your life will never be the same."

He nodded. "I understand. I want to be a Christian."

As we sat in the diner holding hands, I prayed for him while tears of repentance and joy flowed down his cheeks and onto the table in front of us. The customers at the other tables watched in disbelief at this strange sight, two young men holding hands and praying. It's not something they saw every day! But Roberto and I didn't care. We hugged and rejoiced anyway.

SOMEONE JUST LIKE ME

Roberto and I became best friends after that experience. The next day we talked about the Lord during our entire shift. I'd never seen Roberto so happy.

Three days later the hostile foreman started yelling at Roberto for some small infraction, and I decided it was time for both of us to move on.

"Come on, Roberto," I told him. "Let's get out of here. We don't need this job. Now I know why God sent me here—to reach you. And I think it's time both of us moved on to something better."

The foreman looked on with disbelief as the two of us threw our aprons on the table and walked out.

Two weeks later I was preaching at a church and there in the front of the auditorium was Roberto with his entire extended family by his side—twenty-one people in all. They took up the first two rows of the small sanctuary. One by one Roberto began leading them to the Lord over the next few months, until they all came to know Christ.

Roberto later enrolled in a Bible seminary to become a minister. Today, both he and one of his relatives are pastors in California.

I could have never known at the time that God led me to take that job simply as a way of reaching Roberto and his family. The Holy Spirit had been working in his heart for some time, bringing conviction, and all he needed was someone to take him to the next step, someone he could relate to, someone he trusted. Someone just like me—a redeemed sinner.

I hadn't been a follower long enough to know how to listen to the Spirit's leading, but he led me anyway. And if you'll look at your own life and circumstances, you'll see that he's doing the same for you every day.

As Christians, it's our responsibility to watch for those times of nudging, those opportunities to touch the lives of others and pray for the Spirit's help as we respond. For me, that can be in a crowded auditorium or speaking one-on-one with another person.

Throughout my years of ministry and evangelism, God has continued to bring people like Roberto into my life to burn into me a passion for reaching the lost. Through those experiences I've learned to trust his voice, his gentle nudges, as he moves and guides me along the way. At times his requests have seemed strange and awkward, even dangerous, but I've tried to never ignore the Spirit's direction when I feel his gentle nudge.

ORIGINAL GANGSTER

Another of the Spirit's unforgettable confirmations for me of God's call to this ministry came at one of our many hit-and-run outreaches in Houston.

We had set up our lights and equipment in the front yard of a house owned by an elderly Christian woman in the neighborhood—the grandmother-in-law of Dennis Rogers, a professional strongman and the youth pastor of a dynamic church in Houston's inner city. For forty years this gentle woman had served God by living and working in the fifth ward—an area overtaken by drug dealers, gangs, and prostitutes. Though she was an easy target for abuse and violence, the people of the neighborhood respected her, even watched over her, as she daily reached out to the most hopeless kids in the area. If anyone needed food, clothes, or shelter, they could always depend on her for help. It wasn't uncommon to see someone show up on her doorstep with an empty pot. She'd take it back to her kitchen and fill it with soup for them. Several times she risked her life to rescue children from an abusive and drug-infested home. She was God's angel, working and living in a corner of hell on earth.

Dennis was the one who suggested that we hold an outreach at his grandmother-in-law's house, mostly as a show of support for her many years of faithful service to the community.

Often when we set up in a neighborhood, many of the people come because they've heard of me or read one of my books. In the inner city I'm known as an O.G. (an original gangster), a term I seem to be stuck with whether I like it or not. As long as it gets people to show up, they can see me however they choose. But this night, in this neighborhood in Houston's Fifth Ward, I could tell that most had never heard of me. To them we were just a group of street preachers looking for an audience.

As the music started to play, hundreds of people began flocking toward us. It was largely a Hispanic crowd, and many didn't speak English. We were attracting some of the angriest and most troubled teens in the neighborhood, the kids who brought fear into the lives of the others. Several were wearing their gang colors, strutting around the edges of the yard, trying to intimidate us. To one side several Hispanic men were sitting in the back of a pickup truck, drinking and laughing and bouncing to the music.

Our TRUCE workers began fanning out across the crowd, praying and watching for people who might need ministry. Several walked over to the men in the pickup and crawled in beside them. I've always been amazed at the boldness and courage of the kids who help us, many of whom were saved from the streets and now spend their time and energy trying to reach others in the inner city.

I hadn't planned on speaking. Patrick speaks Spanish fairly well and easily connects with an audience, so I try to let him take charge as often as possible. God has chosen to lay his anointing on my first son-in-law, and it's exciting to watch God groom and shape Patrick in his service. When Patrick preaches on the streets, my role becomes one of an intercessor. I pray and watch.

But the Holy Spirit spoke to me on this night and told me to share my testimony, so I took the microphone after Patrick finished. I spoke only in Spanish.

SATAN'S CAPTIVES WALK AWAY

God's spirit fell over the crowd as I spoke. He hit us like a wave crashing upon the shore. Everyone in the audience felt it. As I made a call for repentance, people began rushing forward, weeping under the conviction of the Holy Spirit. Even those who didn't speak Spanish came forward for prayer. They hadn't understood a word I said, but the Spirit moved in their hearts to bring them to conviction.

All the men in the pickup crawled out of it, tossed their bottles aside, and came forward to receive Christ's forgiveness. They were crying like children, begging for forgiveness from their Father. I hugged them and cried with them.

Our TRUCE workers were so moved by this outpouring that they had trouble keeping their composure while praying with people. Many fought to get their words out. All they could do was lay hands on people and cry with them as God ministered through his Spirit.

Several of the kids saved that night were hard-core gang members and pushers. I've always prayed hardest for these kids, because they're the ones who will feel the most persecution for their decision. Much more than the others, they'll be pulled and pressured to turn away from their newfound faith. Often they're risking their lives in making a decision for Christ. But I also find comfort in knowing that God gives these kids a greater measure of his protection and strength to fight the temptations as they come. I know because I've been where they are.

As we prayed and ministered to those coming forward, I noticed pockets of people leaving in all directions. They were strutting away, watching us over their shoulders, anger and hate exploding from their eyes. It's a dynamic that takes shape every time we hold an evangelistic service. When God's Spirit moves in, evil has to flee. Every neighborhood is riddled with a few people who simply refuse to listen, people so entrenched in sin that their hearts are cold and black, especially those who control the drug flow—the pimps and pushers who stand to lose money through our evangelistic efforts. They control the neighborhood through fear and intimidation. Satan's hold is real and definitive, and when God comes near, they flee.

It's for these people that my heart grieves the most. They're so imprisoned by evil, so bound by the chains of hate and deceit and guilt that they can't even recognize the light. Satan has closed their ears to the truth. Someday they'll hit bottom and be ready to listen, and when they do, God will be there to comfort them. But this was not the day.

JESUS UNDERSTANDS

As we ministered to those who had come forward, I saw an elderly grandmother cradling two small children in her arms. She was crying and begging us to pray for her grandchildren.

"Pray that God will protect them," she cried as she set them down. "Please pray that they'll grow up safe and happy, that they won't get into gangs and drugs. Will you do that for me, please?"

The two children clung to her thighs and looked up at me as she spoke, their faces innocent and beautiful.

My heart broke for this woman and her grandchildren. Her eyes cried out for help, for guidance, for any kind of relief from the pain and helplessness of life in the ghetto. I hugged her, then bent down to pray for the children. She continued to heave and sob the entire time.

This is what my life is about, I thought to myself. *This is why I do what I do.* There are so many people in this world who are lost and lonely and hurting, people who have nowhere to turn and no idea how to escape Satan's evil grip. Jesus is the only one who can help them. All they need is someone to point them toward the Cross, someone to care enough to take them by the hand and lead them into the arms of their Creator, someone to hold them and love them into the kingdom.

When I finished praying, I put my arms around the elderly woman and kissed her on the forehead. "Don't worry." I told her. "Everything will be all right. Jesus understands."

There's something about staring into the eyes of hopelessness, of seeing the face of despair, of absolute grief, that brings the gospel message home to you in a way that nothing else can. Your life takes on a renewed sense of purpose and urgency. You begin to despise Satan and all that he stands for: the evil, the hell that he imposes upon others. And you want to spend every waking moment of your life sharing your faith and setting captive souls free.

It's the one thing that keeps me coming back to the streets time and again, day after day, year after year. I see people trapped in sin, suffocating beneath Satan's grip, and I ask myself, *If I don't help them, who will?*

It's a good question for all of us: *If we don't help them, who will?*

CHAPTER TEN

A Great Hope

I'll never forget a meeting I had a couple of years ago with the pastor of a large and affluent congregation. We were planning a TRUCE crusade in his city and were hoping to get help from his church. After I explained our ministry plans to him, he leaned back in his large leather chair, peered at me over the rim of his glasses, and said, "Why would we need to partner with you in this crusade? We already fill our building for three services every Sunday. We don't need any more people."

My mouth nearly dropped to the floor. I never thought I would hear a pastor admit that he's not really interested in reaching any more lost people. I can only assume that he'd rather remain comfortable in his religious bubble, trying to keep his members happy and his job secure.

It's sad enough to see believers in the pews—laypeople—who are apathetic and lazy when it comes to evangelism. But when we see that trait in a pastor, it's nothing short of a spiritual travesty—a mockery of everything Jesus died for.

Nevertheless, in spite of the strong feelings I've expressed about the church's lack of passion for reaching the lost, I'm not interested in pointing fingers or dwelling on the past. The truth is, I have a great deal of hope for the future of the church. With all my heart I believe that this course of stagnation can and will be reversed.

As I travel across this country and beyond, everywhere I look I see signs of revival, pockets of believers who are changing the way they've always believed and taught about God's Spirit on earth. They're calling on the Lord to do great miracles in their midst, and he's answering their prayers.

PLEADING FOR THE SPIRIT

One such church is the Brooklyn Tabernacle, pastored by Jim Cymbala. When Jim took over as pastor of this remarkable church twenty-five years ago, it was a dwindling congregation of twenty members meeting in a run-down, aging building in the heart of the inner city. As the neighborhood declined in value, street gangs and prostitutes began to move in. Few were willing to drive through this dangerous area to attend church, and even fewer wanted to reach out to the undesirable elements around them. So the church began to die, slowly but surely.

After pastoring for two years in frustration, Jim announced to his congregation one Sunday that he was turning the leadership of the church over to the Holy Spirit. He implemented a weekly Tuesday night prayer service. In *Fresh Wind, Fresh Fire,* he recounts what he told them:

> From this day on, the prayer meeting will be the barometer of our church. What happens on Tuesday night will be the gauge by which we will judge success or failure because that will be the measure by which God blesses us.
>
> If we call upon the Lord, he has promised in his Word to answer, to bring the unsaved to himself, to pour out his Spirit among us.... No matter what I preach or what we claim to believe in our heads, the future will depend upon our times of prayer.

Jim and his congregation remained true to that pledge. Each Tuesday night they meet together with one purpose in mind: to plead for the Holy

Spirit to unleash his power on their church and the surrounding neighborhood. That simple act of faith and commitment on the part of God's people has made the Brooklyn Tabernacle one of the greatest evangelistic success stories of our time. Today the church hosts a body of several thousand people, many of whom are former gang members, prostitutes, and drug addicts who have been saved from lives of hopelessness.

GOD TEMPERS THE FIRE

Another example is the Times Square Church, pastored by David Wilkerson, my spiritual father and mentor. Fourteen years ago, while standing on a filthy corner of Times Square in New York, surrounded by prostitutes, drug addicts, and stoned derelicts, he felt the voice of God calling him to move his family and ministry to New York to start a new church. God told David that he would be used to clean up this "heart of Babylon" in the middle of the nation's largest city.

At the time, David was contentedly living and working in Texas, considering retirement and perhaps a new career writing books. But the call from God was undeniable, so he began to pray and seek God's guidance. He pleaded with God to give the vision to someone else, perhaps a younger man in search of a church to pastor. But God continued to wear at David's heart and soul, so he relented and promised to follow, regardless of where this new mission would take him and his family.

If you knew David, you would understand why this calling seemed such a strange fit. No one can argue that David is a powerful speaker and evangelist; when he gets in front of a crowd, God's anointing fills him with the Spirit. I've seen David speak on subjects so controversial and hard-hitting that most speakers would never touch them, yet he always seems to pull it off. He has the ability to bring God's conviction and repentance on even the hardest and coldest crowds. But in spite of this amazing gift, David is not a pastor at heart. Though he served earlier as a pastor for a few small churches, he never felt that this was his strength or calling. But God made it clear that this was what he wanted David to do, so he trusted this mandate and set to work.

Within a few months, the Lord had given David the old Mark Hellinger Theater on Times Square, one of the most corrupt areas of the city. There, with only a handful of faithful supporters and his family by his side, he laid claim to this new vision from God, giving the ministry over to the complete guidance and direction of the Holy Spirit.

Over the months and years to come, I witnessed God shaping and molding David into a pastor. His church continued to grow, and his heart for people grew with it. The man who was once a fiery, hard-hitting evangelist was being softened into a gentle shepherd of souls. The fire was still there, but much more tempered.

Today the Times Square Church hosts weekly services to more than eight thousand people representing nearly a hundred different nationalities. More than two thousand of their members volunteer regularly to work with one of the church's thirty ministries, ranging from feeding and clothing the homeless to ministering on Wall Street. But the backbone of their strength and ministry has always been the Thursday night prayer meetings, where thousands come together each week to call on God's Spirit to work mightily in their midst. "It is the Holy Ghost who has transformed Times Square Church into a missions-focused church," David explains.

This amazing congregation is a living testament to the Lord's power and faithfulness. Through the obedience and commitment of one man, God was able to transform the lives of thousands in this sinful and seemingly hopeless corner of the world. Today Christian leaders travel from all over the world to see firsthand this spiritual phenomenon that God has accomplished through the Times Square Church. And it all began with a simple nudge from God and an act of obedience in the heart and life of one man.

EVEN IN A HARDENED PLACE

Also in New York, in one of the most hardened neighborhoods in Queens, God is unleashing his power on the young people of the community through the ministry of Christ Tabernacle, a dynamic congregation that has consistently made an impact for Christ in their community.

This church is pastored by my good friend Michael Durso. Under his leadership, the congregation daily spends itself on behalf of the poor and helpless, ministering to the needs of the neighborhood.

Four years ago, Michael's son, Adam, was called by God to oversee the church's youth department. At the time they had eighteen young people attending regularly. The Holy Spirit planted a fire of evangelism into this small group of kids, and they envisioned reaching their entire community for Christ. They began meeting every Friday night to pray and plead with God to release his Spirit through them. They committed to fasting and praying on a weekly basis in an effort to hear God's leading. Each one began inviting friends from their schools and neighborhoods to this Friday night gathering that they called Aftershock. Every week the attendance grew and more kids were getting saved. By the end of their first year they had more than 250 kids attending their Friday night services. They named their ministry Youth Explosion, which is entirely appropriate. Their success is extremely unusual for the New York area. Most church youth groups there are doing well to get 30 or 40 young people involved.

I've been privileged to spend a lot of time with Adam's group through the years, speaking and ministering at every opportunity. Their enthusiasm and devotion to the Lord never ceases to move and inspire me. It's exhilarating to see so many kids on fire for Jesus. I've met with Adam often to express my support and admiration for his commitment to these kids and their neighborhood.

Several years ago I encouraged him to begin integrating the youth group into the church body. I felt that the kids were becoming too much of a church unto themselves, separate from the older members. And I knew that in order to feel united as a church body they needed to meet together weekly. Adam took my advice and began bringing the kids into the services every Sunday, where the group sits front and center. The older members began mentoring the younger ones, helping them grow and mature in the Lord, the way God intended.

The group met each Friday night for prayer and worship, and the kids continued to reach out to their schools and neighborhoods. Many of the kids they were bringing in were gang members, prostitutes, and homeless teens from the area. But every week saw more kids turning away from sin and making a commitment to Christ. The kids built a large Plexiglas box and placed it in the corner of their meeting room in the church basement; newcomers were encouraged to use it to discard those evil reminders of their old life. The box began to fill with gang colors and flags, gangster CDs, knives, guns, drug paraphernalia, cigarettes, magazines, anything that represented a life under the bondage of sin and Satan. With each meeting the box filled higher as more kids came under the conviction of the Holy Spirit.

Soon they had a core group of four hundred committed kids, each continuing to reach out to their friends and neighbors. Their Friday night services became so popular that the YMCA down the street from them started losing business, and they wondered why their building was so empty during what used to be their busiest hours of operation.

One Friday night the young director of the YMCA paid a visit to their meeting to see what was going on. He intended to confront Adam and try to convince him to change his meeting time so that they could recoup their lost business. Instead, the kids drew him in and welcomed him as a friend. Before the night was over, this man found himself in tears in front of the group, praying for repentance and giving his life to Christ. He has now become a regular part of their youth group.

Today the church has a core of five hundred committed kids and usually hosts a crowd of around seven hundred each Friday night for their prayer and worship services. Most of these kids come on their own, since their parents (if they're around) often don't attend church. Since their first meeting four years ago, they haven't had one gathering without someone's giving their life to Christ.

While most youth groups across the country are busy entertaining kids with skating parties and skiing trips, these dedicated kids spend their times together feeding the homeless, evangelizing in the streets, and praying for revival. And the Spirit is using them to make an eternal impact on their community and the world.

WILL WE TAKE THE PROMISED POWER?

Jesus promised the release of his power and the Spirit on the lives of his followers, to move among them with signs, wonders, and miracles that would leave no doubt about his power in the eyes of a lost and hopeless world. He promised to send his Spirit to live among and inside them, to guide them as they took the gospel to every corner of the globe. He assured them that his Spirit would never leave or let them down, and he expected them to put total faith and trust in this "still, small voice" guiding them in their hearts.

The prophet Joel foretold this power that would manifest itself upon followers of Christ. "I will pour out my Spirit on all people. Your sons and daughters will prophesy, your old men will dream dreams, your young men will see visions. Even on my servants, both men and women, I will pour out my Spirit in those days. I will show wonders in the heavens and on the earth" (Joel 2:28-30).

We have before us an opportunity to see the Lord's might loosed on the world as never before. God is ready and willing to pour out his power, to perform miracles in the name of Christ the likes of which haven't been witnessed since the resurrection of Jesus. But when and whether he decides to do that through our lives depends on whether we're willing to step out of our comfort zones, to reevaluate the way we think and believe, to forsake the things of this world, and to trust instead in God's promise of provision.

Are we willing to put aside our own opinions and agendas and focus instead on the leading of the Holy Spirit?

Will we choose to believe in a big and powerful God?

the holiness

Among those who approach me
I will show myself holy;
in the sight of all the people
I will be honored.

LEVITICUS 10:3

Who can stand in the presence of the LORD, this holy God?

1 SAMUEL 6:20

The LORD Almighty is the one you are to regard as holy.

ISAIAH 8:13

When they see among them their children,
the work of my hands,
they will keep my name holy;
they will acknowledge the holiness
of the Holy One of Jacob,
and will stand in awe of the God of Israel.

ISAIAH 29:23

Christ Jesus…through the Spirit of holiness was declared with power to be the Son of God by his resurrection from the dead: Jesus Christ our Lord.

ROMANS 1:1,4

immersed
in one mission

After nearly forty years in God's service, watching the Holy Spirit move before me with one miracle after another, seeing the Lord's hand so clearly in my life and ministry, you'd think I'd be accustomed to the way he works. Yet still I marvel at the gracious way he continues to make known his awesome power, a power that truly sets him apart in holiness.

When God redirected me in my ministry eight years ago—through the angelic visitation in Mexico and further guidance that followed—I could look back on abundant and dynamic examples throughout my years of ministry of how the Spirit's power works on earth.

The most helpful way I know to reveal this to you is to take you back to these days and to let you see what he was teaching me.

That was when I was a young follower of Jesus, a new husband in my early twenties, working and living in the same area where Satan once held me captive. My entire life was immersed in one mission—to help others out of the same hopelessness and despair and sin that I once knew. God used those years to bring me to total brokenness before his throne, to completely redirect my life and heart. They were the most frightening yet glorious years of my life.

BROUGHT TO SHAME

Only a few months after I returned to New York from attending Bible college in California, I was preaching one evening at a church in the Bronx. At the time a lot of preachers seemed more concerned with how people dressed and acted—matters of personal choice with only external significance—than with whether people had a heart for God. I found myself getting caught up in the same concerns.

I was speaking at one of the largest churches in the Bronx, and the place was completely packed. I had prepared a lesson that was sure to get their attention. I preached against every sin I could think of. I slammed men for having long hair and unkempt beards, and for wearing torn jeans and long beads around their necks. I spoke out against women who wore short skirts and tube tops and heavy makeup and expensive jewelry. I left no stone unturned. By the time my tirade was over, I was sure that I had offended every person in the auditorium.

After thoroughly berating the crowd, I decided to use the last few minutes of my sermon to share my testimony. I found it hard to concentrate, because a lot of people were getting up and walking out, but I continued nonetheless. I was sure God was pleased with my boldness. *People need to hear the truth,* I thought to myself, *even if they don't like it.* It didn't occur to me at the time that the people who were leaving were the ones who most needed Jesus. They were the sinners Jesus had sent me there to reach.

I had a surprisingly small response to the altar call that day, but I didn't worry about it too much. I prayed with the people who came forward, then went to my car, pretty proud of myself for the hard-hitting lesson I had delivered.

During the drive home I remember being completely happy and content with my performance. I was singing along with the radio and thanking God for the people who had come forward for prayer. I was looking forward to my next sermon, wondering if there was any sin I had forgotten to expose. Then suddenly, just as I reached the Brooklyn Bridge, the Holy Spirit hit me with a powerful wave of conviction and guilt. It seemed to come out of nowhere. One minute I was blissful and pleased, thrilled with myself, and the next I was in complete horror at what I had done. It hit me like a brick. *What was I doing?* I thought to myself. *How could I have been so cold and callous? That's not what I was called to do?*

In my heart I could hear God saying to me, "Shame on you, Nicky. This isn't what I saved you for. You've wounded a lot of people tonight. I didn't call you to condemn people; I called you to tell them I can save them, like I saved you. You would never have come to me if David Wilkerson had spoken to you the way you spoke to those people tonight. You came because he loved you and because I loved you.

"From now on I want you to preach me, and me alone. Tell people how much I love them. Tell them about my son, Jesus."

I was so ashamed. I began to pray aloud, "Dear Jesus, please forgive me. I will never speak like that again. Never will I condemn people for their sins. From now on I will only talk about you and your love."

To this day I've never forgotten that promise I made to my Savior. And he has never failed to be faithful in helping me reach those who need him.

DETERMINED TO BREAK THROUGH

A man named Raymond was someone God used early in those years to show me the Spirit's miraculous and holy power.

There was something about Raymond that always bothered me. He had an elusive way about him, like someone with a secret to hide. He was a good-looking kid: tall, thin and muscular, twenty-four-years-old, with a clean complexion and a ready smile—something of a charmer. When you asked him a question, he was quick to answer and seemed comfortable making conversation. Still, there was a subtle vagueness about him, something I couldn't quite put my finger on.

I first met Raymond while I was serving as director of the Spanish program for Teen Challenge in New York City. I was fresh out of Bible college at the time and had been a Christian for only four years. Gloria and I were newlyweds, and Teen Challenge was my first calling into hands-on street ministry. It was David Wilkerson, my spiritual father, who first asked me to take on the role as director of the center. He wanted a ministry that would take up where he left off, preaching in the streets and ministering to the most violent and helpless in the city. Gloria and I moved into an apartment above an old garage behind the Teen Challenge Center, and we set to work, not knowing what to expect but trusting God to lead.

Raymond was just one of the many drug addicts on the street who came to us looking for help. I could tell he was high the first time he stepped through the door, though he didn't seem desperate or out-of-control. He asked for assistance, so we made up a bed in a corner of our center and took him in.

At the time we also had a number of other people from the streets staying in our center. We had addicts, homeless teens, prostitutes, and gangbangers, each of whom had come to us looking for sanctuary or a place to dry out from the drugs ravaging their system. I never had the heart to turn anyone away, so even though our center wasn't intended as a shelter, it became something of a halfway house.

Through the weeks, Raymond became the topic of many discussions. The others in the center didn't get along with him. They told me they didn't trust him—that he seemed to be up to something. Several asked me to send him away, but I wasn't ready to give up on him. Something in my spirit told me to stick with him, to let him stay.

In a strange way, Raymond reminded me of myself. He was hard to reach and completely unresponsive to the gospel. He wanted help with his drug habit, but he didn't want to accept Jesus. I stuck with him because I could see through the walls he'd built around himself. I was determined to break through to him, though he continued to resist my attempts.

"I'm Begging You"

One Sunday morning, while getting dressed for church, Gloria and I heard a knock on the door to our apartment. It was Raymond.

"Nicky," he said, "I need to talk to you."

"I'd be glad to," I told him, "but we're on our way out the door. Can this wait until later?"

"No, it can't, Nicky," he answered, with desperation in his voice. "I need you to come to the Bronx with me."

I tried to explain that we were on our way to church and even offered to let him wait in our apartment while we went. "We'll go after I get home," I told him.

But he persisted. "Nicky, I'm begging you. This is a cry from my heart. Please take me to the Bronx right now. I really need you to do this for me."

I continued to ask him what was wrong, to tell me what he needed so I could better help him, but he wouldn't say. He insisted that he simply needed me to go with him. I explained my dilemma to Gloria and asked her to take the subway to church and allow me to help Raymond. As always, she understood.

Raymond led me into the worst section of the Bronx, with glass and bricks littering the streets all around. It was an area they called Fort Apache. Several looted and burned-out cars sat on the side of the road. It looked like a war zone. He took me to the front of an old, dilapidated building and told me to pull over. It looked condemned, and I was convinced Raymond had led us to the wrong place.

"Are you sure this is the right building?" I asked him. "This place is empty."

"This is it," he replied, emotionless.

"No one could possibly live here," I told him. "You must have the wrong place."

"I know where I am," Raymond insisted.

He got out of the car and led me up a back stairwell to the second floor, then down the hall toward the end. As we walked, we stepped over broken bottles, dried urine, and rotting bags of trash. A rat scurried around the corner ahead of us. The stench was unbearable. I held my sleeve over my nose to keep from throwing up.

"What are we doing here, Raymond?" I asked. "There's no one here."

"Just follow me, Nicky."

He opened the door to an apartment and stepped inside. The room reeked of urine and liquor and waste. There was no furniture, just more trash and debris covering the floor. Flies were everywhere. Inside stood a young woman, half-naked, staring out the cracked opening of an outer window. She was holding a tiny baby in her arms, naked, dirty, crying from hunger. Beside her on the floor were two children, a boy and a girl. They sat motionless, eyes downward. The young girl was wearing nothing but a filthy diaper. I wondered how long it had been since she'd been changed. The woman turned to face me. Her eyes were black and hollow, void of emotion. Dried dirt and makeup smeared the sides of her face. Her clothes were filthy and her hair was matted.

Raymond turned to me, tears flowing down his cheeks.

"This is my sister and her kids," he said through sobs. "I'm so embarrassed that you have to see this, Nicky. She's retarded and can't take care of herself. I'm the only one left to take care of them, but I can't do it anymore. I can't even stay clean!"

Raymond crouched to the ground and began weeping uncontrollably. I tried to comfort him, but the sight of this woman and her children in this den of filth overwhelmed me. I just sat and cried with him.

"Don't worry, Raymond." I said. "We'll take care of this. I'll help you."

The woman turned again to face the outside window. She rocked back and forth, holding the baby tightly in her arms as it cried. The other children grabbed her by the legs and held on tightly.

"How did this happen, Raymond? Where is your mother? Can't she help your sister?"

Raymond didn't answer. He just continued to sob.

We spent the rest of the afternoon getting the woman and her children cleaned up and fed. Gloria called a local hospital to help, and they brought in some people from social services to take care of the family and find them a place to stay. It took some talking to convince Raymond that this would be best.

"I KILLED MY MOTHER"

Later that evening, I sat with Raymond in my office.

"Raymond," I said, "why didn't you tell me about this sooner? Why don't you open up and tell me what's going on in your life? We can help you. That's what we're here for."

"I'm sorry, Nicky," he said. "It's just so hard." He leaned back in his chair and took a deep breath. Through his tears he began to tell me his heart-wrenching story.

"My mother used to take care of them, and I was always out running around, getting stoned, and stealing. I didn't want to stay home, so I roamed the streets. I was always in trouble, and it broke my mother's heart. I loved my mother and didn't want to hurt her, but I just couldn't stand to be at home. I wouldn't listen to anything she said. My two older brothers got involved with a street mafia and it got them killed. They were found hanging in an empty building on Coney Island. Mom didn't want me to end up like them, but I didn't care.

"One day I got caught stealing and had to go to jail. I was in for over a year. As soon as I got out, I went crazy and got high. I didn't learn a thing. I was still running the streets, drinking, doing heroin, and mugging people. I came home one day to find my mother crying. I remember it was on a Thursday. She was waiting for me. She had a butcher knife in her hands, and when I walked in the door she lunged at me and pushed me against the wall. She tried to put the knife in my hand and was screaming at me. 'Why don't you just kill me? I can't stand what you're doing to me and this family. I've already lost two sons to the streets, and now you're bent on getting yourself killed, and I can't take that! I want you to kill me right now! Take me out of my misery!'

"I told her not to talk like that, that I loved her and wouldn't do anything to hurt her. I cried and gave her my word that I would stop. I told her I wouldn't steal anymore, and would stop doing heroin. I promised her. And I meant it.

"She looked at me and said, 'Raymond, you have my word. If you ever go to jail again, I will kill myself. You will never see me alive again.'

"In my heart I knew she meant it, and I truly intended to change. And for a few months I did. But then I ran out of money and couldn't stand being sober, so I robbed a liquor store and got caught. They sent me back to jail.

"I had only been in jail for three days when a chaplain came by my cell. He sat me down and said he had some bad news. Before he even got the words out, I knew what he was going to say. My mother had made good on her promise. She had committed suicide.

"At that instant I went crazy. I couldn't stand the thought of my mother dying. I began tearing my cell apart. The chaplain ran out of the cell and quickly locked the door behind him. I kicked and slammed everything in sight. I tore up my bed, my mattress, the sink and toilet, ripped up my sheets and clothes—anything I could get my hands on. Nicky, I was like a wild animal, and I couldn't stop. The guards couldn't get me to stop, so they just stood outside my cell waiting for me to run out of strength. Later they had to tie me down in the corner in order to clean up the mess.

"Nicky, I killed my mother! All I had to do was stay out of trouble and stay sober, and I couldn't do it!"

Raymond bent over in his chair, buried his face in his hands, and sobbed. My heart hurt for him. I hugged him and prayed with him for the rest of the evening. He cried until he had no tears left.

"Nicky, please help me change," he said. "I'll do whatever it takes, just please help me."

WOUNDS THIS DEEP

I bent down beside Raymond and looked into his eyes. I can't remember the last time I felt so helpless and inadequate. How do you help someone like Raymond? What could I possibly say to make the pain go away, to salve wounds that run this deep and wide—wounds that have literally scarred a person for life? Silently, I prayed for wisdom.

"Raymond, I have to be honest with you. I don't know what to tell you. I'm not equipped to help you deal with your pain. All I know is that you have to come the way I've come. You have to take your problems to God. I know you're hurting, I can feel it, I can see it in your eyes. But I can't help you. Only Jesus can. I'll do what I can for you. I'll hold you, I'll cry with you, I'll stay with you as long as you want. But what you need, Raymond, is Jesus."

He sat staring out of a small opening in the window above my desk. His eyes were red and moist, and his lip began to quiver once again.

"Nicky, I know you're right. Would you pray for me?"

For the first time since I had known him, Raymond was opening up to God. I laid my hands on his shoulders and began to pray.

"Dear Jesus, you know how much Raymond is hurting. You understand his pain. You know what he is going through. Please touch his heart and take away the sorrow. Show him your love and gentleness. Have compassion on this child who needs you so much."

Tears once again welled up and flooded down the sides of Raymond's face. "Do you want to ask Jesus into your heart?" I asked him.

"Yes, I do, Nicky," he told me.

Together we prayed as Raymond accepted Jesus as his Savior. Afterward we hugged and cried together awhile longer.

"Thank you, Nicky. I don't know how to be a Christian, but I'll do the best I can. Will you help show me what to do?"

"You know I will, Raymond." I assured him. "I'll help you. And Jesus will help you as well. We'll go through this together."

Over the months and years to come, I watched God do a miracle in Raymond's life. He was turning Raymond into a new creation, one step at a time. Though I was young in the Lord myself, I began to disciple him, to study with him, to pray with him each day. With the help of Jesus, I mentored Raymond and watched him grow in Christ. He kicked his addiction to drugs and learned how to stay obedient to God. I saw the change in his life as Jesus continued to minister to his heart and spirit. Before long Raymond became one of our most compassionate helpers. He went to visit his sister and her children often, helping them every chance he got.

A few years later we helped send Raymond to Bible college. Raymond finished his studies and went into the ministry, and today he's still working tirelessly to help the poor and homeless. His life is a powerful testament to God's amazing love and his willingness to forever change a person's heart and future.

CHAPTER TWELVE

More Miracles, More Brokenness

During those years as director of Teen Challenge, I saw God work miracles in the lives of countless lost souls like Raymond. God used this time to shape me, to teach me his ways, and to disciple me in his service.

This was long before most of the world had heard of Nicky Cruz, before the national exposure brought on by *The Cross and the Switchblade,* before the books and the television appearances, before the crusades and filled stadiums. Back then it was just Jesus and me, walking together in this new life he had given me.

I had no real skills and no idea where my newfound faith would take me, just a burning desire to love and serve my Savior. I depended on Jesus for everything—my food, my shelter, my rent money—everything. And he never let me down. That was a beautiful and precious time in my life as a young follower of Christ, learning daily how to listen to God's Spirit and follow wherever he might lead.

OFFENDED—AND HELPLESS

As I followed the Spirit's guidance, the first person in New York that I set my sights on reaching for the Lord was a man named Sonny Arguinzoni. I met him through one of the volunteers in our center. Sonny wasn't like other kids from the street. He was polite and well groomed, from a good Christian family. But he had a serious drug problem he couldn't shake. Drugs had often landed him in trouble, and he'd been in and out of several prison hospitals trying to get free of his addiction, but nothing seemed to work. Sonny didn't deny that he had a problem, but he couldn't imagine that God could help. One day God put it on my heart to challenge him.

"Sonny, whether you admit it or not, you have a problem, and Jesus is the only one who can help you. You're no better than the addicts on the streets. If you don't do something about it, you're going to end up just like them, in the gutter or dead. If you had any guts, you'd let Jesus come in and help you."

Sonny was offended by my comments and let me know it. In my heart I knew God would deliver him if he would only open up and let him.

As we talked, I could see in his eyes that he was higher than ever. I challenged him to let Jesus heal him of his addiction.

"I wish I could believe you, Nicky," he said. "I want to be free. But you can't help me. No one can."

I knew that if something didn't change soon, Sonny probably wouldn't live to see his next birthday. I sensed that God wanted me to help Sonny then and there—that tomorrow might be too late. So I went to Gloria and told her not to expect me home for a few days, then I took Sonny to a room on the third floor of our apartment building. I locked the door behind us.

"Sonny, give me just three or four days, and I promise God will deliver you from your drugs. I won't leave you alone. I'll stay here with you the entire time."

"I want to believe you, Nicky," he said through tears, "but I've tried before and no one can help me. I hate drugs. I hate what they're doing to me.

But I can't live without them. You can't help me, Nicky. You're just wasting your time."

WHITE AS SNOW

I wasn't going to give up on him. "Jesus can help you, Sonny. Trust me, and I'll help you get clean. Just give him a chance."

There were two small beds in the room, so I pulled one toward the outside wall, just beneath the window, and the other I pushed against the door leading to the hallway. I lay Sonny on the bed by the window, then sat on the one by the door.

"If you want to leave this room," I told him, "you have to go through me. And I'm not letting that happen until you come down from your drugs and accept Jesus as your Savior."

For the next hour Sonny screamed out in pain. Over and over he slammed his fist against the wall, desperately struggling for relief. I prayed for God to bring him comfort, but the drugs continued to rage within him.

Several times he tried to get up and walk around the room, but his legs would buckle. The drugs had sucked the strength from his body.

At one point, he gasped, holding his stomach with both hands. "I need something, Nicky! It hurts! Help me, Nicky."

"I know it hurts, Sonny, but you've got to hold on. You've been high for too long. It's time to come down and let Jesus save you."

He begged me to let him go. Once he reached over and opened the window beside his bed. "If you don't let me out, I'm jumping out of this window," he said. "Don't think I won't do it, Nicky!"

I stood my ground. "You could do that, Sonny. But if you do, I hope you break both your legs, because then I can drag you back up here and you won't be able to fight anymore. You'll be stuck with me for a long time."

He lay back on the bed and began to cry. I walked over, laid my hand on his shoulder, then prayed for him. "Dear Jesus, please help my friend Sonny.

Take away the pain. Take away the desire for these drugs that are killing his life and keeping him in bondage. Show him your love and forgiveness. Help him understand how much he needs you. Jesus, show Sonny your power and your strength over this evil that plagues his life."

For the rest of the night and through the entire next day I sat on the bed by the door while Sonny writhed in pain. The drugs in his system wouldn't allow him to sleep or eat.

By the end of the second night I could barely keep my eyes open. Though I tried my best to stay awake with Sonny, fatigue finally got the best of me and I fell asleep beside the door. The last thing I remember hearing was Sonny's sobbing, begging for relief from the pain.

The next morning I awoke to the sight of Sonny standing over me. He was smiling and happy.

"Nicky, look outside," he told me.

The sun was shining and the streets were covered with a bed of fresh, white snow. It was as bright and beautiful a day as I had seen in years.

Sonny was crying as he stood beside me. The pain was over. "God did it, Nicky. He cleaned me up and saved me. I asked him this morning to come into my heart, and he did. My heart is clean and white, just like the snow outside!"

Tears were running down his face as he hugged me.

"I feel so pure, Nicky. God has forgiven me; I know he has. I'm free. I don't ever want to go back to my life of sin and drugs!"

It was a wonderful time of rejoicing for Sonny and me. He was my first converted drug addict at Teen Challenge, and he began working beside Gloria and me as we reached out to the lost of New York. Sonny was my spiritual son, and I mentored him in the Lord through the next few years. He soon became my right-hand man, and he never lost his passion to preach about Jesus. So many times I remember Sonny's saying to me, "Nicky, I love Jesus so much, I just want to tell everyone about him. I want to bring the whole city of New York to Jesus!" God's Spirit burned within his heart and soul.

Some years later, Sonny married a beautiful Mexican girl named Julie, and together they founded Victory Outreach in Los Angeles. Today that ministry has helped thousands of people throughout the world, and Sonny and I continue to be the best of friends and co-laborers in God's kingdom.

ON THE STREETS OF HARLEM

Each new day at Teen Challenge brought a fresh understanding of God's holy and awesome power. We began preaching and ministering in the streets wherever God would lead.

We could feel the power of God's Spirit as we walked through the streets of Harlem, telling people about Jesus and preaching the gospel message. People from all races and nationalities were receiving our words, often hearing the good news for the first time and giving their lives to Christ. These new converts were on fire for the Lord, and each night they joined us as we moved through the streets, preaching God's love and forgiveness.

We began breaking up into groups, penetrating all areas of the inner city. Jesus' love and forgiveness had planted a deep burden for the lost within the hearts of these new converts, and they couldn't wait to bring all their friends to salvation. Each time a new person would come to Christ, the others would surround them, imparting Christ's love within them. They became one of us. Their hearts were broken and vulnerable before God, and Jesus became their first love.

We saw some of the coldest, hardest people on the streets break down before us under the conviction of the Holy Spirit. Gang leaders, lifelong criminals, prostitutes, pimps, drug dealers, and hard-core heroin addicts—all were feeling the supernatural moving of the Spirit and giving themselves over to the love of Jesus. Many would come to us after years of living in the streets, immersed in a lifestyle of drugs, violence, and immorality, and Jesus would set them free. We would take them back to the center with us and help them dry out from the drugs and alcohol ravaging their systems. Then we would mentor them in their new walk. Soon they, too, were working alongside us in our ministry to the lost and hopeless.

What we experienced during that time was a faith in Christ as pure and powerful as anything I had ever witnessed. We were completely committed to the Spirit's leading, never questioning his ways or his wisdom. We couldn't wait to get up each morning to see what new miracle God was going to do in our midst.

We truly believed that if we remained faithful to God's Word, he would pour out his Spirit on our lives and ministry. We prayed for hours on end that he would use us to further his kingdom. We would drink of God's Word, focusing on the life and ministry of Jesus, praying that God would impart in us that same power and compassion. As we read of Jesus' healing the lepers, we pleaded with God to help us heal the lepers of New York City. As we studied the stories of Jesus' casting out demons, we would drop to our knees and claim authority over the demons in our midst. We claimed the promise of Jesus to Martha—that if we believed, we would see the glory of God (John 11:40). And he never let us down. God continued to manifest his power in our midst.

As we preached and ministered on the streets, more and more people were coming to us for spiritual and emotional healing, often showing up on our doorstep looking for help. We rounded up blankets and mattresses wherever we could find them, and soon all three floors as well as the basement were filled with people drying out from drugs or looking for sanctuary from the streets—from their pimps, their gangs, their pushers. Every room and hallway was filled with mattresses and sleeping bags. I had to step over several people in my office just to make it to my desk to make a phone call. Our entire budget went to feeding and ministering to these poor people, and many times we wondered where the next dollar would come from. But we committed to never turn anyone away, and God continued to provide.

Once I sent Sonny with a group of people to conduct a street outreach in Harlem. I stayed at the center, and within a few hours Sonny and the others came home with a large group of street addicts who had no place to stay. Several were high on drugs, and Sonny had brought them all back so we could help them. I was shocked to see so many and wondered where we were going to put them all.

"There'll be another group along in a little while," Sonny said. "We didn't have room for them in the vans, so I gave them some money to take the subway." Sure enough, about forty-five minutes later, another eight or ten people showed up on our doorstep looking for help.

Sonny would become so excited about helping people that he often got carried away with compassion. But God always seemed to help us find a way to deal with anyone who came to us needing help.

HOLY GHOST HOSPITAL

God's compassion flowed powerfully throughout our Teen Challenge center as we continued to disciple God's new converts in their newfound faith. Each day started with two hours of Bible study and prayer. We read stories from the Old and New Testaments and taught about Jesus. We were teaching them how to live a life in the Lord, how to combat the sinful temptations brought on by Satan, and how to share their faith with others. They continued to ask what they could do to help, so we taught them how to love and encourage each other.

Everyone in the center fasted and prayed one day a week for our work with the lost. In the beginning I fasted two days a week, but it soon wore down my defenses, and Gloria convinced me that once every seven days was enough.

The presence of God was so strong and real among us that everyone felt it. Each time we had visitors, they found themselves completely taken by the powerful presence of the Holy Spirit. So many people talked of the discernible sense of love and goodness that permeated every hallway of the building. Many were brought to tears just by standing in the presence of God's glory at 416 Clinton Avenue.

God's compassion flowed through us and into the people we were ministering to. When they saw a friend struggling through the pangs of withdrawal, they would sit beside him and hold a wet, cold towel on his forehead to bring the fever down. They wept with each other and prayed for God's comfort when they saw their friends hurting.

God was changing hearts and lives daily. People who had spent most of their lives thinking only of themselves were now becoming new creations, filled with the compassion of Jesus.

During those days, we were just servants to the Holy Spirit's work. He was the director of our center. We were simply the nurses in God's "Holy Ghost Hospital," and Jesus was the surgeon. Every time the doorbell rang, we knew God had sent another soul needing help.

At times it felt as if Luke were writing about us when he described the early days of the first church:

> All the believers were one in heart and mind. No one claimed that
> any of his possessions was his own, but they shared everything they
> had. With great power the apostles continued to testify to the resur-
> rection of the Lord Jesus, and much grace was upon them all. There
> were no needy persons among them. (Acts 4:32-34)

Like the early church, we found strength in love and fellowship. We were one in purpose and faith, and God used our unity in spirit to bless and heal, to draw even more people to himself. Our faith was infectious.

So many times I would be awakened at one or two in the morning to someone's cries of anguish and loneliness. I'd make my way downstairs to find a person on a cot in the hallway, writhing in pain, desperate for relief from the drugs infiltrating his system. Many nights I would be on my knees cleaning up someone's vomit on the floor. I would spend hours holding him and praying for him, crying out for God to bring him comfort. Often God would place his hand on a heart and soothe the pain, putting the hurting soul back to sleep. Other times God would allow him to suffer through the process. I never questioned God's decision; I just trusted that he knew what was most needed at the moment. I comforted people the best I could.

SCREAMING FOR RELIEF

A writer who was doing research on our ministry once came to us, and as he sat in my office, I could tell he was uncomfortable with the people stretched out on the cots just outside the office. He kept glancing over toward the doorway, distracted by their presence.

Suddenly a long and guttural cry came from the hallway outside the office. A person new to our center was drying out from drugs, and his pain was becoming unbearable. He was screaming for relief. I walked out the door, knelt down beside him, and placed my hand on his forehead. Then I began to pray: "Dear Jesus, give this poor soul some relief from his pain. Don't let him suffer any longer. He can no longer bear this pain. Breathe your peace into his spirit and let him sleep."

Immediately the man's face became calm and the shaking stopped. He lay back against the mattress and closed his eyes, breathing a deep sigh of relief. His arms fell to his sides, and within minutes he fell asleep.

The writer stood watching in amazement. He couldn't believe the miracle he'd just witnessed. "How is that possible?" he asked me. "How do you make a person's pain go away like that? Is there some trick to it, like some kind of hypnosis?"

I explained to him that it was God who soothed his spirit, not me, but I could tell he was skeptical. I had become so accustomed to the Spirit's work among us that I often forgot how strange and unbelievable such things appeared to others.

BROKEN AND STRIPPED OF PRIDE

More than any other time in my life, those years I spent with Teen Challenge shaped my view of ministry as well as my relationship with the Lord. I saw God working among us in ways too powerful to possibly describe in words. So many lives were touched by God's love and provision. And through it all, Jesus continued to hold my hand, to mentor me, to teach me his ways and the depth of his compassion for others. I had no way of knowing how much those years would affect my life and future. God was grooming me for a lifetime of service.

Still today I can remember the cries of agony that flowed through the hallways of our Teen Challenge center, the groans of addicts fighting the pangs of withdrawal, struggling to find some comfort from the pain. It was the sound of total and complete helplessness, a soul in bondage to sin, yearning, begging to be set free. Satan had grabbed them by the heart and was now fighting to hang on, torturing them relentlessly, desperate not to let go.

So often these people had nothing left to give and nothing to live for. Satan had stolen their jobs, their families, their wives and kids, their dignity, their hope. And now the only thing left to take was their lives. He had succeeded in stripping these poor souls of everything they'd ever had or cared for, and now he sat back and laughed as they writhed on the floor in pain. Our job was to take them back, to give them back the love and dignity they needed to survive, to snatch them out of the jaws of hell and place them into the arms of Jesus.

I long for every follower of Christ to see firsthand what I saw at the center. I wish you could see the pain, the helplessness, the loneliness. There's something about holding a hopeless person in your arms that moves you to compassion and brings you straight to the very heart of Jesus. When you're on your knees on the floor, mopping up the vomit left by a person you just met, a person who has lost all sense of dignity and self-respect, you begin to understand what it means to be a servant of the poor and sick and needy. You begin to see people the way Jesus sees them and to love them the way he has loved us all.

And you get a small glimpse into the true consequences of our sin, of selling out to Satan, of listening to his lies and giving in to his temptations.

To this day I loathe Satan with all my being. I've seen his methods, his ways. I've witnessed his hate and contempt for God's children, for all that is good and lovely in the eyes of the Lord. He'll stop at nothing to deceive and win a soul, to beat a person into submission and condemn him to the same hell that he is forced to suffer. And because I've seen it, I will spend the rest of my days fighting to thwart his evil attempts.

My years at Teen Challenge were some of the toughest and most challenging days of my life, but they've made an everlasting impression on my heart. God used that time to completely break me of my prejudices against others. I've learned that God's love and compassion knows no boundaries, no skin color, no race or background. Where I once saw black, white, Asian, or Hispanic, I now see only children of God.

And he also stripped me of my pride. There was a time in my life when pride was everything; it was all I had and all I thought I ever needed. Before God could use me, he had to break me down, to strip away the arrogance and self-sufficiency of my past, to make me a servant of those I once despised. Only then could I begin to understand the compassion and humility of Jesus.

Walking in the Spirit demands brokenness. If we want to hear God's voice, to feel his leading, we do it through complete humility and dependence. If we want God to teach us his ways, we must first stand in total submission to his holy will.

It's only through service and surrender that we find true joy and freedom in Christ.

power on display

When I left Teen Challenge in the fall of 1964, it was as much a leap of faith as when I had first taken that position several years earlier. The one serious regret I had about my time there was the strain it put on my marriage. In my enthusiasm for God's work I had often ignored Gloria, leaving her home alone for long hours during the day while I worked at the center, then spending many of my nights preaching and ministering in the streets. There was always so much to do and never enough time, and I threw myself headlong into the work, not understanding how lonely it must have been for her. She always seemed to understand and seldom complained.

It was only when I decided to leave my work at the center and move back to California that she opened up to me about this frustration in her life. We'd recently had our first little daughter, Alicia, and Gloria let me know she expected to see more of me if we were going to raise a family. I knew she was right. And that was one of the primary factors behind our move.

AN ETERNAL INVESTMENT

Several months earlier I had learned that a handful of the people at our center were looking for a way to further their study of God's Word. A couple of them were praying that God would help them find the funds to attend college. One day they came to me asking for guidance. "If this is God's will," I told them, "then he will find a way to make it happen. Continue to pray about it, and I'll do the same."

God put it on my heart to ask my good friend Kathryn Kuhlman, a prophetess and minister whom I'd met through my outreach. Kathryn had become a close friend to our family through the years. She was a kind and sensitive woman who loved God deeply. I remember her coming to the center once, holding my little daughter, Alicia, and praying for her often. She used to bring gifts to Alicia every time she was in town.

Kathryn preached every week to thousands of people in auditoriums in Youngstown, Ohio, and in Pittsburgh. She often would invite me to come speak for her, and I was always happy to help when I could. She found out once that I had a weakness for strawberries, and many times I would receive a huge package filled with strawberries—a gift from Kathryn. She used to shower my family with gifts, and once she even bought me my first tailor-made suit. When I needed a car, Kathryn was there to give me the down payment. There was nothing she wouldn't do for me, and I grew to love her dearly.

What I appreciated most about Kathryn was the way she ministered to the people at our center. Several times she came to speak to us, laying hands on the sick and healing them. To this day I've never met a person with such a powerful anointing by God to heal.

Once she came to speak to the men at our center and noticed a man leaning against a wall in the hallway. He was a drug addict who had come to us for help. But he had no interest in hearing about God. He simply wanted to dry out and be on his way. The man had no way of knowing who Kathryn was or why she was there. And she didn't know anything about him. But as she passed him in the hallway, she stopped suddenly and turned to face him. She placed her hand on his head, and immediately the man's knees buckled and he fell to the floor. She continued to pray for him, but he couldn't move. He was completely immobilized by the power of the Holy Spirit. Kathryn finished praying for the man then casually went on her way as he lay still on the floor. It was a powerful thing to witness.

I knew that if anyone could help these men go to college, Kathryn could. So one day when she was in town I decided to ask.

"If you want to make an eternal investment," I told her, "help me send these kids to college. It will be an investment in their future and in the work of the Lord. We have thirteen men who want to go into the ministry. I can't promise that all of them will make it. In fact, I'm sure some of them won't. But even if one person comes through and makes an impact for the Lord, it will have been worth the time and money. Won't you consider helping us?"

Kathryn didn't hesitate. She committed on the spot to sponsoring all thirteen of the men to attend the same college I had attended in California. That was another catalyst for our decision to move back to the West Coast—so I could keep an eye on them as they continued their studies. It eventually proved to be a fruitful investment. Seven of the men went into full-time ministry and pastoral work. Two of the others have died, while the rest have remained faithful to God in career fields other than full-time ministry.

DOUBT AND DISCOURAGEMENT

It was on the long drive to California that I felt my first rush of doubt about this new endeavor. I suddenly realized that I had just cashed my last paycheck and had nothing lined up for the future. Gloria and I had very little savings, and I knew that something had to happen quickly. The reality of being unemployed weighed heavily on my heart through the entire trip. Though I trusted God to provide, since he always had in the past, I still struggled with a sense of anxiety and fear.

I knew I would have offers to speak. The book based on David Wilkerson's experiences in New York, *The Cross and the Switchblade,* had recently been released, and I had been in demand since. But for some reason I shied away from accepting money when I spoke. Before, when people offered to pay me,

I always refused and had them make out a check to Teen Challenge instead. I'd always chalked it up to humility, but in my heart I knew it was my proud Latino heritage coming out. I was adamantly against taking handouts. Somehow, in my mind, taking money for speaking seemed to be an admittance of hardship, and I never wanted anyone to think I needed help. In spite of all God had taught me about humility, I still struggled with pride in some areas.

I was planning on continuing in the ministry, doing whatever God called me to do, and while driving cross-country in our first car, Gloria and I dreamed aloud about all the wonderful ways we would serve. But I still felt the need to pay my own way. Gloria and I would both find jobs, she in an office and I working with my hands, and we would commit our evenings and weekends to God's work.

I've always loved the Bay area, and moving into our small apartment in Oakland gave me a fresh sense of excitement for this new chapter of my life. But as the weeks went by, our enthusiasm waned. No job offers came, and our money was dwindling quickly. We prayed daily for God to bring an offer for work, but it never came. We found homes for most of the young men who had moved to California to attend school, but two of them had to stay with us for a while. Alicia moved into a corner of our bedroom to make room for everyone. Gloria worked hard to see that we all had food, but our funds were tight and it wasn't easy for her.

One day I was sitting at the small table in our apartment, eating a bowl of cold cereal for lunch, feeling as low as ever. We had six dollars in the bank and still no work lined up. I couldn't understand why God had forgotten about us.

Suddenly the phone rang. It was the pastor of a church in Castro Valley who said he'd just learned that Nicky Cruz was in the area. "You're the same Nicky that's in the book, aren't you?" he asked hesitantly.

I assured him I was.

He asked if I'd be willing to speak to his congregation of around seven hundred people. "We can't pay much, but it would be a great honor," he said.

I immediately agreed. *Finally, we'll get a little money in the bank,* I thought.

Gloria seemed surprised when I told her about it later that evening. "I've got nothing to say right now, but I'm going to do it for the money," I told her. "I don't know how much they're willing to pay, but whatever it is I'll take it. I'm sick of being so poor. If they're willing to pay me, I'll go and tell my testimony."

NOTHING TO SAY

The meeting was on a Wednesday night, and the building was packed with people. All the seats were filled, and extra chairs were brought in and lined around the walls of the auditorium. I knew my appearance would bring in a decent crowd, but I never expected this type of reception.

Sitting on the front row of the sanctuary, listening to the music and waiting for my turn to speak, a sudden wave of guilt and remorse ripped into my heart. *What am I doing here? How could I have let myself stoop this low? I don't have anything to say to these people. I don't even want to be here. I've got no business telling anyone about my relationship with God. Especially when I've never felt so far from him. This is wrong. There's no way God will bless this service. I should just get up and leave.*

I struggled to hang on to my composure. I considered walking away, telling them that I didn't feel well, that I'd come back to speak at another time, but I knew I couldn't. People had come to hear me speak, and as wrong as it seemed to talk in my frame of mind, it would have been an even worse witness to leave them hanging. "Dear Jesus," I prayed, "forgive me for coming here. I know I shouldn't have come. But please help me get through this evening. Give me something to say that will be worthwhile."

As I stood up behind the podium, looking out over the smiling faces of people eager to hear my testimony, I struggled to get the words past my lips. My interpreter was a man named Jeff Morales, and through him I started to share my testimony, as I had done so many times before, but my heart wasn't in it. I was empty. My words were cold.

I stopped and stepped around the pulpit to the front of the stage. "I have to be honest with you," I said. "My motives are not pure. I came here tonight because we need the money, not because I have something to say. I've been trying to fake it, but my heart won't let me go on. I can't do that to my Jesus. I love him too much. I've asked him to forgive me, and I hope you will forgive me too."

Tears were running down the sides of my face as I broke down and shared my failures. I wondered how the crowd would react to this disappointing revelation. As I looked up, I saw a number of people in the crowd sobbing with me. A voice from the back carried over the crowd, "We love you, Nicky."

A sea of tears began to fall as people continued to encourage me from their seats.

"I don't know if I can get through my message," I said. "But if you'll bear with me, I'll try to go on."

With my heart in my hand, I continued to share my testimony. The longer I spoke, the clearer my mind seemed to become. God was helping me speak.

I finished my testimony, then made a halfhearted call for repentance. I was just glad to be through with my talk and honestly didn't expect anyone to come forward. But one by one, people began moving into the aisles and toward the front, mostly teenagers. People were weeping and kneeling before the altar. Soon the entire front of the auditorium was packed with souls crying out in repentance. Many in the back were on their knees praying. I had never before been in a service where the Spirit of God moved so mightily in the hearts of people.

God was speaking to me through this miraculous event. He was showing me that even though I had let him down, even though I had let my poor motives and attitude get in the way of my service to him, he was still on his throne. Though I was empty and felt far from him, he was right there beside me all along.

Though I was expected to pray for the people coming forward, I couldn't bring myself to do it. Instead I walked down in front of the altar and fell on my knees beside them. "Thank you, Jesus," I cried. "Thank you for your love and faithfulness. Forgive me for being so weak and faithless."

A PROMISE OF THE SPIRIT'S PRESENCE

That night I recommitted my heart and future to God. "I don't know what you have planned for us," I told him, "but whatever it is, I promise to trust you. I won't doubt your hand in my life again."

The pastor paid me seven hundred dollars for my appearance. It was more money than I had seen in weeks. Though I still struggled to accept it, I knew God had orchestrated this evening as a show of his provision, so I swallowed my pride and pocketed the money.

In the car on the way home, Gloria and I were filled with excitement over what God had done. "Let me take you out to eat, Gloria," I said. We hadn't been to a restaurant in months, and I wanted to do something nice to celebrate. "Let's not go home," I told her. "Let's drive to San Francisco, to that place in Chinatown you like so much. Let me take you out to eat for a change!"

We felt like two kids on their honeymoon as we drove, the windows down and the radio tuned to our favorite station. I pulled Gloria over next to me and put my arm around her shoulder as we cruised down the highway. We were laughing and joking and snuggling as we drove. But by the time we reached the bridge leading into San Francisco, our conversation had lulled. Everything was quiet. Suddenly it hit me how selfishly we were acting. I looked at Gloria and said softly, "Let's go home. We don't need to go out and eat. We need to be thanking God for this gift he's given us."

Gloria smiled and nodded in agreement. By the look in her eyes I could tell she had the same thought.

We turned around and went back to our tiny apartment. Together we knelt beside the bed. "Sweet Jesus," I prayed, "thank you for being with me tonight. I'm so sorry I doubted you. And I'm sorry for my pride. I know you're true to your word, and that you would never let us starve. Thank you for this glorious provision you've laid in our laps."

We spent the next two hours crying and praying together, praising God for his goodness. In my spirit I felt God speaking to me. *Nicky, you have been faithful to me, and now I will be faithful to you. You have been tested and you still remained true to my love. I've showed you my power and my compassion. You know my heart. From this moment on, I want you to trust me for everything; I will supply all your needs. I'm going to raise you up as an evangelist of my Word, of my grace and mercy. Your past will bring glory to my kingdom. My Spirit will always be upon you, and my hand will follow you wherever you go.*

It wasn't an audible voice, but I knew it was from God. It was a covenant of trust between a Father and a son.

I've never forgotten his promise, and he's stayed true to his word ever since.

Today I'm in my fourth decade of preaching and sharing my testimony in countries all over the globe, and I have never once made a call for repentance without seeing a lost soul come to Jesus. God's Spirit has been with me every time I've stepped forward to speak and share my faith. At times I've felt all alone, wondering if he was there, sensing that my words were not connecting. Other times I've spoken when I didn't feel I had anything to say. But God's holy power always shows up in spite of my doubts and weaknesses. He's never let me down.

To a New Level

Gloria and I both knew what God wanted us to do. If he'd wanted us to have a job, he could have easily given us one. Instead he wanted us to throw ourselves into ministry and trust him to provide. And he blessed us beyond our wildest dreams.

From that moment on, the phone never stopped ringing. I continued to get offers to speak, and I went wherever God sent me. I was speaking in auditoriums and stadiums all over the world, especially in England and Europe.

I remember speaking at the Royal Albert Hall in London and looking out over a sea of faces. More than nine thousand people attended that day. A few hours before the crusade, my interpreter had called and said he couldn't make it, so I was forced to speak the best I could in English and hope that the people could understand. The Spirit of God intervened and drew people to himself, helping them understand my words in spite of my poor English. It was an overwhelming experience for me.

I discovered that during this new chapter in my life, God wanted to take my faith to a new level and to mentor me even deeper into his glory. At Teen Challenge, God had taught me how to serve others. He had instilled within me a deep love and compassion for the lost. I'd seen the pain and damage that sin and illicit sex and drugs bring into a person's life and the hopelessness of living without God, and I never wanted to see another person go through that kind of agony. I was on a mission to lead every soul I came into contact with into the arms of Jesus. He also demonstrated his power and authority over evil and the full depth of his grace and mercy. I'd seen what God could do in the life of a helpless, hopeless soul. He had broken me of my prejudices and my pride and taught me the virtues of humility and brokenness.

And now God wanted to show me just how big and powerful he was and how willing to move and work through me if I would just turn loose and allow him to do so.

Every time I spoke, God increased my boldness and faith. He continued to show me his power. I began to feel I could do anything in the name of Jesus.

AN AFRICAN DOWNPOUR

Once I was speaking at a crusade in South Africa. It was something of a miracle that I was even allowed to speak at the time. I had been openly critical of the government and had often taken a stand against apartheid in media interviews. Just a few days before the crusade, I had blasted the government of South Africa for allowing this class distinction between blacks and whites to continue and grow. I even warned openly against a revolution if the injustices continued. But the media was on my side, so the government left me alone.

I was to speak at an outdoor stadium, and the night of the crusade the rains began to pour. The clouds moved in and wouldn't let up. The closer time came to start, the harder it rained, and by the time people had filled the stadium, we were in the middle of a downpour. Workers quickly erected two large umbrellas over the stage area in an effort to keep the speakers and sound equipment dry. Huddled together on the floor of the arena were thousands of people, standing in the rain, getting soaked to the skin. And there was no sign that it was going to let up.

Gloria and I were in a secluded room high above the stadium floor, looking out over the masses huddling together in the rain. It broke my heart to see them getting drenched, but I knew God wouldn't want us to cancel the event. My book *Run Baby Run* was extremely popular in South Africa, and many nonbelievers had come to hear me speak.

From this vantage point above the gathering crowd, I got a good look at them. Everyone was white! I couldn't see a dark-skinned person anywhere in sight, except for Gloria and me. My mind immediately raced back to the comments I had made just a few days earlier, and I honestly felt a bit tense over the prospect of facing this crowd, but God calmed my spirit.

When it came time for me to speak, a volunteer led me down a long staircase in the back of the stadium and through a hallway to the floor of the stage. Before going out, I told some workers to move the umbrellas away. "If these people are going to stand in the rain to hear me speak, I'm going to get wet with them," I said. They quickly disassembled it, and I stood a safe distance away from the microphone to keep from getting shocked.

As I walked out onto the stage and faced the large crowd of people, compassion filled my spirit. The rain beat down so hard that I knew they would have trouble hearing my message. Suddenly, in my spirit I sensed God's telling me to pray for relief from the downpour, so I did.

"If everyone would bow with me, I'd like to take a minute and ask God to stop this rain," I said.

I began to pray. "Sweet Jesus, you know we love to see your beautiful rain, but there are people here who don't know you. They know who I am, but they don't know you. Give them a chance to listen to your word, to hear your gospel. Please stop this rain so I can share your good news with them. I know that you control the weather, that you are in control of everything, but many here have never seen your power. Show them your might. I'm going to do my best to give my testimony, to tell of what you've done in my life. But first, please stop the rain. Thank you, Jesus, for answering this prayer."

In a sudden burst of boldness, I cried out, "Jesus, stop the rain now!"

As soon as I finished, a loud clap of thunder rang out, and the rain started to slow. Within thirty seconds it had stopped completely. The crowd stood in astonishment. For the first minute there was a rumbling of whispers moving through the stadium, then all became quiet and every eye focused forward.

At that moment I understood completely why God had placed in my spirit the desire to pray. People had come that night to see Nicky Cruz, the kid from *The Cross and the Switchblade* and *Run Baby Run,* the former gang member turned preacher. But now the focus was on God Almighty!

That night I saw a greater outpouring of repentance than I had ever witnessed. So many people came forward for prayer that we had no way of getting around to them all. The crusade workers and I stayed for hours afterward laying hands on people and praying with them for salvation and healing. No one wanted to go home. Thousands had witnessed the power of God, and not one person—skeptic or believer—was left unaffected by it.

The story of God's miraculous intervention ran in newspapers throughout the country, and for years afterward we received letters from people who had come to Christ as a direct result of these miracles. If there were any doubt before about God's sovereignty, it was more than dispelled.

GOD'S REASON FOR DISPLAYING HIS POWER

In the third chapter of Acts, after Peter and John had healed a crippled beggar at the gate leading into the temple, a number of onlookers stood in amazement at the sight. They had known the man for years, and the healing was undeniable. When the people questioned the disciples about it, Peter said to them, "Men of Israel, why does this surprise you? Why do you stare at us as if by our own power or godliness we had made this man walk? The God of Abraham, Isaac and Jacob, the God of our fathers, has glorified his servant Jesus" (3:12-13).

When God decides to display his power in the presence of unbelievers, he does it for a reason. The intent is to glorify Jesus, to draw people to himself, to give us a small glimpse of what heaven is going to be like, of the amazing possibilities that lie ahead for those who choose to serve him. He's displaying his complete and encompassing authority over the natural world. When he chooses to do that, it isn't our part to question or manipulate the situation, but only to accept it and to give him the recognition and praise he deserves.

Sadly, I've found more resistance to God's supernatural power from within the body of Christ than from outside of it. It's usually the believers who are skeptical. They've not seen God working such miracles in their own lives, so they doubt that he does so in the lives of others.

I used to spend a lot of time worrying about this, trying to correct these attitudes. But now I choose to just push forward, to continue ministering and preaching and moving in God's Spirit, and to let others believe what they want. If they seek God's power and Spirit, he will reveal it to them. It's not my role to argue or try to change their minds.

Still, it saddens me to see so many followers missing out on the joy and power that Christ could bring into their lives if only they would open up and accept it.

open to God's supremacy

In my life and ministry I've seen that the more willing I am to open up to God's supremacy, the more willing he is to display it. I've learned to never try to box him in or second-guess his ways.

And when a supernatural God does business in a natural world, no one in his path goes away unaffected. That truth hit home to me in a way I will never forget during a two-week evangelistic crusade in South America.

HUNDREDS OF WITCHES

We were in Asunción, the capital city of Paraguay, during the first night of a four-night evangelistic crusade. The stadium was the largest in the country, seating more than forty-five thousand, and we expected to fill it to capacity.

I stood staring up into the clear sky, looking beyond a large red billboard perched high above the west edge of the stadium. Far in the distance I caught a glimpse of a huge black cloud moving toward us. It seemed to come from nowhere.

"I thought the weather was supposed to be nice today," I said to a ministry volunteer standing next to me.

"It's not supposed to rain," he answered, squinting tightly to get a better look at the cloud. "The news said clear skies all day. Looks like they were wrong."

I looked at my watch. Fifty-five minutes until start time. *Maybe the cloud will turn,* I thought. The stadium was already beginning to fill with people, so I made my way toward a holding room in the back to make some final preparations. Workers were scurrying about in all directions.

As I walked, one of the event coordinators ran to catch up with me. "Nicky, the witches are here," she said, a little out of breath.

"Where are they?" I asked.

"Everywhere," she answered. "Mostly they're outside the stadium, but some are inside, in the bleachers and hallways!"

"How many?"

"We're not sure. Two, three hundred maybe."

I glanced overhead. The cloud loomed closer, almost directly above the stadium, darker than before. Otherwise the sky was clear and blue. I stopped and looked at her. "You know what this is, don't you?"

She nodded. "I think I do."

"We need to pray," I said. "Tell the others, we need to pray *now!*"

She took a deep breath and ran ahead of me toward the coordination room beneath the bleachers. I began interceding as I walked: "Jesus, give us strength and power and authority over the evil that surrounds us. Bind Satan in our midst!"

To one side I noticed two women standing next to a chain-link fence. They were witches, each wearing a long white robe tied at the waist. One was smearing blood on a corner of the stadium wall with her hands. The other turned toward me, and I could see rows of animal bones and teeth strung tightly into a rope hanging from her neck. She held a long staff high in the air, and her eyes rolled back into her head as she stood and chanted. Suddenly she dropped her arms and looked directly at me, hate exploding from her eyes as she glared. Her stare followed me as I continued to walk and pray.

Passing the rear entrance to the stadium I caught a glimpse of the traffic winding along the road leading into the parking lot. Cars were backed up for miles. The bleachers continued to fill as people poured in through every entrance. "Dear Jesus," I prayed, "we haven't got much time. Fill us with your power and authority! Give us victory over this evil presence."

I knew we were in for a long night of spiritual warfare.

CONSTANT BATTLE

Since our arrival in South America three days earlier, we'd been in a constant battle with the spiritual forces of evil in the area. Before our trip we'd learned that more than two thousand witches and satanic priests from all over South and Central America had convened in Paraguay and planted themselves in different parts of the city, praying against our crusade. And they were committed to remain throughout the duration of our stay. We had brought with us about seventy-five prayer warriors from the United States to intervene on our behalf. We knew early on we were in for a fierce battle.

From the moment we stepped off the airplane, the presence of evil was almost palpable. Satan's stronghold was real and decisive. You could feel it in the air. But God was not to be outdone.

As we arrived at the hotel, the lobby was already filled with hurting and lost people looking for prayer. They flocked toward us from all directions, hungry to hear about Jesus. Before we could even check into our rooms, we spent hours sharing with people, laying hands on them, and leading them in prayers of repentance.

That afternoon, as I walked down the street with a handful of volunteers by my side, a crowd gathered around us and begged for prayer and healing. We stood on the streets until late in the evening, ministering, interceding, healing, convicting, and laying hands on people as God poured his power through us. Though we had a schedule to keep, it became apparent from the first hour that we were no longer in control. God had another agenda in mind. Once again we were transported by God, walking through the pages of the book of Acts, moving and working within his might and power, following as the Holy Spirit led.

Well into the night, and for the next two days afterward, we continued to minister as people came to us pleading for help. We learned that the government of Paraguay had taken notice of our presence and had begun showing the film *The Cross and the Switchblade* during prime time on national television. They aired it for three consecutive nights leading up to our crusade. As a result, people flooded into Asunción from miles around in an effort to hear God's Word.

Every evening we ministered until all hours of the night wherever we happened to be—in shops, in restaurants, on street corners, in the stadium. Many of the hotel staff and cleaning people came to the Lord. I barely had time to eat or sleep. I found myself having to sneak away to my hotel room for a quick snack and a thirty-minute nap, then the phone would ring and I was up again, meeting more people in the lobby for ministry.

The frustrated witches and satanic priests continued to pray against us throughout the entire ordeal. Everywhere we went, we saw them cowering in the shadows, always at a safe distance, pleading with Satan to thwart our efforts, wondering why their prayers went unanswered. As always, God was winning a clear and decisive victory.

Still, the evil one wasn't going to give up easily.

DISTRACTED BY DANGER

In the stadium, as the black cloud hovered above us, I stood on the floor beneath the stage as the announcer welcomed the crowd and thanked everyone for coming. "We've been told that this is the largest crowd ever to gather in this stadium," he said to a roar of shouts and applause. The stadium was filled beyond capacity, and many were turned away at the gate.

Meanwhile, the strange cloud had planted itself directly overhead. A number of people in the stands were looking up, pointing toward the sky, wondering and worrying.

"Do you think we should have canceled?" I heard someone say behind me. "If there's lightning, this could be bad. There's not enough shelter for everyone."

I turned to see several of our volunteers talking among themselves, anxiously looking at the cloud.

"Listen," I said to them, "right now is not a time to worry. You need to be praying. God is not going to let Satan ruin this night. It is not going to lightning; it's not even going to rain. God will part these clouds. But I want you to gather up the others, find a quiet place, and pray. We will not be overcome!"

They left together quickly as the announcer introduced me, calling me onto the stage. "Dear God, you know what needs to be done," I prayed. "And I know that you're in control. Give me strength once again as I speak on your behalf."

I had been working on a book about witchcraft and Satanism, and the message I had prepared was about standing against the evils of the occult. My intention was to challenge Satan in his own backyard, to expose the dangers of Santeria and black magic, to explain Satan's hold on those who delve into these seemingly harmless practices. Since beginning work on this book about Satanism, I had felt Lucifer's attacks on my life and ministry. This night was no exception.

As I stood and shared my message with the crowd, I could feel my throat constrict and dry up. I struggled to get the words from my brain to my lips. I'd never felt such a strange sensation. Normally I find speaking rather comfortable, but this night was different. I couldn't get my words to make sense, and I could tell I was losing the crowd. Several times I heard thunder overhead, but I continued to speak, praying for God to work through me, to break this hold Satan had on my tongue. People were distracted by the danger looming above us, and I fought to keep their attention. But I persisted in speaking and praying for God to work.

TIME TO TAKE CONTROL

Suddenly, halfway through my message, a ray of light shone through the middle of the cloud. Slowly the thunderous swirls of darkness began breaking apart, floating piece by piece into the distance. Within fifteen minutes the cloud was completely gone, and the bright South American sun shone hard on the stadium. At the same time, I found my voice, and the thoughts began to flow. Once again, the Holy Spirit was beginning to pour his words through me and into the hearts of those in attendance.

As I began calling for repentance, a flood of souls poured into the aisles and toward the front. Men and women fell to their knees under the Spirit's conviction. Before long, thousands had come forward to receive Christ. Our volunteers were overwhelmed by the response, so I called for Christians in the stands to come forward and help us minister and lay hands on the people coming for prayer.

I was on my knees on stage, praying for a couple of young boys who had come forward, when one of the volunteers ran toward me from the back of the stage. She was in a panic.

"Nicky, the witches are going crazy. They're all over the place, cursing and hitting people. They're furious. There's no telling what they're going to do."

I rose to my feet and looked out over the crowd. A tide of holy anger began welling up within me.

I walked to the back of the stage, where a handful of our volunteers were standing. "I don't want anyone to be afraid," I told them, "but we are under Satan's attack here tonight. His witches have been here all night praying against us, and now they are angry. I've been patient, and God has been patient, but now it's time to take control. We need to pray right now!"

We gathered in a circle as I prayed. "Dear God and Creator of the universe, take dominion over this place. Satan has had his fun. Now it is time to bring him to his knees. In the name of Jesus I command every evil force in this stadium: Leave! You are not welcome here. We will no longer tolerate your subversive attempts. You have no power and no authority over this place. I command you to stop in the name of Jesus Christ! By the blood of Jesus, we rebuke you. Out!"

PIERCING CRIES

At that moment a mass of cries began piercing the air from every direction. All over the stadium the witches were falling onto the ground, convulsing, gasping for air. A few of our volunteers cautiously approached several of the trembling people writhing on the floor. One woman lay on the floor next to the stage, screaming out in pain. I made my way to the floor and began laying hands on as many as possible, praying for Satan's hold on their spirits to be released. From outside the stadium came piercing sirens of several ambulances, and soon paramedics began rushing toward the crowd. They reached down to help one man writhing in pain, convulsing on the floor.

"Leave him alone," I told them. "God will deliver him. He'll be okay."

I bent down and prayed for the man. Suddenly he became calm, and his heavy breathing subsided. A paramedic shone a light in his eyes and checked his heart with a stethoscope. Several other witches stopped screaming and began breathing steadily as volunteers prayed over them. Before long, most had been delivered from the evil in their spirits and were walking calmly about the stadium, dazed and confused. A few dozen were unaffected by our prayers and were loaded into the ambulances and taken to a nearby hospital. Others ran from the stadium in horror as soon as they made it to their feet. A few of them stayed among us, weeping, as volunteers witnessed to them and led them in prayers of repentance.

We stood in awe as eyewitnesses to God's holy authority and might.

More than nine thousand people received Christ that evening. Over the next three nights around eighteen thousand more came to Christ in Paraguay as word of the miraculous events spread through the country, bringing more lost souls looking for salvation. God continued to go before us, leading with his Spirit, guiding us to those who needed his touch on their lives.

From there we went to Uruguay and Argentina for another ten days of ministry and healing. Through the entire trip the Spirit never left us. Everywhere we went, hundreds would follow, mobbing us, asking about Jesus. Thousands more were brought to Christ through the conviction of the Holy Spirit.

ALMOST PARALYZED

At the end of the two-week tour, I found myself heading home, physically and emotionally exhausted. I'd had very little sleep and had eaten little during the entire period. I could tell I had lost a lot of weight by the way my clothes were fitting. Still, the exhilaration of the Holy Spirit inside my heart and soul was overwhelming. I could hardly sit still. I was addicted to his presence and power, drunk with his spirit. I didn't want to leave South America. It was an amazing and humbling experience, and I didn't want it to end. Quite honestly, I had become spoiled and didn't want to come down from this spiritual high that God had given me.

When I arrived home, I hugged and kissed Gloria and my children and began telling them of the miraculous works God had done in our midst. They were excited for me, and we prayed together, thanking God again for his mighty victory over evil. Still, I found it frustrating to try to express the true depth and power of my remarkable experiences in South America. I knew I could never fully describe the extent of God's anointing during my time there.

For several days I walked around the house almost numb. On the outside everything seemed fine. Life was carrying on as usual. But inside I sensed a deep depression settling into my spirit. The third day after my arrival home, I could hardly make it out of bed. I crawled to my feet and retreated to the downstairs family room, where I lay on the couch, emotionally exhausted. When Gloria called me to lunch, I told her I wasn't hungry and continued to lie and rest. I had work to do at the office, but I couldn't muster the energy to go. Gloria was convinced that I was coming down with something, so she took my calls and told me to rest for a while. In my heart I knew it was something very different.

For the next two days I remained on the couch, almost paralyzed by depression. I couldn't eat. And I couldn't shake my feelings of despair. I felt completely detached from Gloria and the kids, from my work, from the outside world, and from God. I prayed that he would release me from this sense of helplessness. More than anything I longed for the might and power that I'd experienced in South America. I felt that he had deserted me, left me to fend for myself. For two weeks I existed solely on his presence and strength, feeling him near. And now I was left alone. I'd had a small glimpse of heaven, a taste of it, and now I wanted more. I even prayed for God to take me home, to take me out of this world and into his arms, but he remained silent. I was like a baby taken from his mother's breast, longing for the sweetness of her milk, her fragrance, her comfort.

Several times I got angry with God. I didn't think it was fair for him to take me into such deep communion with himself—to show me so much of his glory and presence—and then desert me like this.

Gloria started to worry. Over and over she tried to get me to eat, but I couldn't. She tried praying with me, but it didn't seem to help. After three days of isolation, she finally came downstairs, angry and determined to shake me out of my sadness.

"Nicky, what's the matter with you? Why are you doing this to us? Why are you doing this to yourself?"

I didn't know what to say.

"The kids and I feel like you're not even here. You're gone for weeks at a time, and now when you do come home, you're too tired to even talk to us. This isn't the man I married. I can't stand to see you this way! Why are you acting like this?"

Again I wasn't sure how to answer. "I'm trying to snap out of it, Gloria, but I just can't." I tried to explain my feelings to her. I told her how I felt abandoned by God and that I was ready for him to just take me home. "I'm sure I'll get over it in time. But right now I don't have the energy to argue. I'm so tired. I just want to sleep."

WAITING FOR ME

Gloria stood for a few moments looking down at me. I could tell she wasn't happy. She might easily have gone back upstairs and left me alone to wallow in self-pity, but she loved me too much to leave at that moment.

"Nicky," Gloria said, "you know I love you, but I don't accept this. God doesn't accept this. You can't spend your life like this. Satan is attacking you right now, and you need to fight him back."

She walked over to the couch, laid her hands on my head, then began to pray. She took authority over me and my depression. I was surprised at the boldness in her voice.

"Jesus, you need to give Nicky back his strength. You need to come into his spirit and renew him. Make him come out of this feeling of despair, make him eat and be happy again. Sweet Jesus, we know you can revive his soul, and we beg you to do so. Don't let him stay like this. Bring him back to us. Please, Jesus! Give him back his desire to live and work and love again."

She sat beside me, kissed me on the forehead, and took my hand in hers.

"Nicky, I'm going upstairs now. I'm not going to beg you anymore to eat. In a little while, I want you to come upstairs and be with me and the kids. We need you, and you need us. I'll be waiting for you, Nicky."

I'd always known Gloria was a strong woman, but I tend to forget just how much I love and need her. After she went upstairs, I lay on the couch for another two hours. I could feel the strength coming back into my heart and soul.

Finally, I got up and pulled on my clothes and made my way upstairs to the kitchen. Gloria had a bowl of chicken soup waiting for me. She smiled and kissed me on the cheek as I walked into the room.

"Thank you, Gloria," I said. "I'm sorry for the way I've been acting. I hope you'll forgive me."

She sat me down and poured me a large cup of hot soup without saying a word. Somehow I knew she understood.

After years in public ministry, I've learned a stark lesson: Satan has a way of attacking us where it hurts and when we're most vulnerable. When we allow ourselves to be used by God in such powerful ways, we can always expect Satan to be there, hiding in the shadows, waiting for an opportunity to trip us and make us fall.

Thankfully, God is always there to pick us up and to work through those closest to us to renew our strength and spirit.

Satan may fight and claw and attack, but he can never conquer!

CHAPTER FIFTEEN

God Hasn't Changed

As I travel across the country speaking and evangelizing, I've found myself at more and more large and affluent churches, mostly because of the success of our outreach programs. The Christian community has taken notice, and many are wondering who we are and what we're all about. I accept many of these invitations in spite of my busy schedule, because I never want to miss an opportunity to share Christ's power with others.

When speaking, I often tell stories that illustrate God's work within our ministry, like the events I just shared about our crusade in South America. I tell a number of other stories as well. I tell of hardened criminals and gang leaders coming to our crusades with the intent of causing trouble, but instead finding themselves convicted by the Holy Spirit and falling to the floor in tears, asking God for forgiveness. They turn their lives over to God and often bring their friends and families with them to the next evening's rally. By the time our next crusade comes to town, many of these new Christians are working alongside us as we try to reach even more people for Christ.

Other times I tell of miraculous healings—both physical and spiritual— that take place during our street-side services. I tell of addicted drug users who have spent years trying to get sober. Often they've been in and out of rehab clinics trying desperately to get clean, yet they continue to go back to their old habits. Someone from our staff will lay hands on them and pray over them, and within minutes the Holy Spirit comes in and takes away the desire. No pain. No withdrawals. Just a new lease on life and a deep desire to love and serve God.

There are children, crippled from birth, who come to our rallies and go home a few hours later, walking and leaping with joy. I tell of abusive and alcoholic fathers who leave our crusades free of their anger and frustration, never again to pick up a bottle or lift a hand against their loved ones. I tell of couples who come to us on the verge of divorce, harboring years of hate and resentment toward each other. They leave with a deep sense of forgiveness and a renewed vision for their marriage. Each of these people comes looking for help, and they find healing in the arms of the Holy Spirit. Their lives are never the same.

WHY DON'T WE SEE IT?

Almost without fail, after I share these testimonies to the Spirit's power, people come up to me with amazement in their eyes. "I can't believe how miraculously the Lord works in your ministry," they tell me. "I've never imagined that God works that way to bring people to Christ."

Then come the questions that inevitably follow. "Do you really think God works the same way today that he did in the New Testament? If so, why don't we see him working in *our* church that way?"

The answer to the first question is easy. "Of course he does." I tell them. "I see it every day. Since the day I became a Christian I've seen no distinction between what I read about in the book of Acts and what I experience in my ministry."

The second question gets a bit stickier—more personal. The risk of offending people is pretty high. But I've never been one to shy away from the truth, so I usually say what's on my mind. "Perhaps the reason you don't see God doing mighty works," I tell them, "is because you don't really believe in a mighty God. He doesn't work miracles because you don't expect him to."

My listeners usually take a step back.

"Or maybe," I continue, "it's because your purpose in asking doesn't impress God too much. Maybe you're spending more time praying to be blessed than you are in asking God to help you bless others."

It's not the answer they expect, but it usually gets their attention.

UNCHANGING GOD

The truth is, God has not changed. He's the same yesterday, today, and forever (Hebrews 13:8). The Holy Spirit who walked with the disciples through the pages of Acts, healing and casting out demons in the name of Jesus, is the same Spirit whom you and I walk with every day. Jesus called him our "Counselor" (John 16:7). Paul described him as an "intercessor," here to help us in our weakness and to walk alongside us (Romans 8:26).

Jesus also spoke of the power that will be imparted to his followers when the Spirit comes: "I tell you the truth, anyone who has faith in me will do what I have been doing. He will do even greater things than these, because I am going to the Father" (John 14:12). And in his last words to his followers before being taken up into heaven, Jesus spoke again of the mighty things we will do in his name: "But you will receive power when the Holy Spirit comes on you; and you will be my witnesses in Jerusalem, and in all Judea and Samaria, and to the ends of the earth" (Acts 1:8).

Do we really understand the implications of such a promise? The Lord tells us that planted deep within the soul of every believer is a piece of God, a small measure of his majesty, a portion of his strength and power. It's like a holy fire raging within us, waiting to be set free, desperately yearning to be loosed on a lost and hurting world, to bear witness to the full might of God's wonder and glory.

Yet how seldom we attempt to tap into that power. Instead we choose to let it simmer, keep it covered, quench it, and in some cases allow it to extinguish altogether.

Make no mistake: The Spirit of God is alive and working in the world today with all the magnificence and authority he displayed in the days of the first-century church. Through the help and influence of the Holy Spirit, God has empowered his people to do greater and mightier acts in the name of Jesus than most of us could ever dream or imagine. He hasn't changed, even if we have. I see evidence of that truth every day in my ministry. And it seldom comes in the form we expect. God is much more creative than we are, and he continues to work in ways that surprise us, particularly in regard to spiritual battle with the enemy.

Make a Serious Assault

I've been known to say (usually during one of my more frustrated moments) that most believers today wouldn't know a good spiritual battle if it bit them on the behind. More than a few times I've had Christians take me aside and question me about the stories I tell—stories of satanic oppression, demonic strongholds, physical and spiritual healings—stories similar to the ones I've shared throughout this book. They've never seen such things, and I suppose they wonder if my testimonies about them are valid. I could try to prove the accuracy of these events, perhaps by putting them into contact with the people who witnessed them firsthand. I could even carry with me the hundreds of letters and newspaper clippings we've collected in our office that give eyewitness accounts of these supernatural manifestations of God's power. But I don't.

Instead I simply lean in close and tell them, "If you want to see the power of God's Spirit come alive in your presence, just make a serious assault on Satan's territory in the name of Jesus. Then you'll see for yourself the wrath of Satan's demons and the manifestation of the Holy Spirit's authority over them!"

Most people are surprised—and offended—by this comment. They assume they're already making an assault on Satan and an impact on the world for Christ. Maybe they are. But my experience tells me that when Satan feels threatened by you—you'll know it.

MY FAMILY UNDER ATTACK

Some years ago I was holding an evangelistic crusade at one of the largest churches in Puerto Rico, and God told me to speak on the subject of witchcraft and the occult. People who delve into black magic and sorcery don't want to believe that their superstitions and practices are actually opening a doorway into evil and demonic regions. They don't like it when I tell them that engaging in the occult is a form of Satan worship, but it is. It's anything but harmless.

More than three thousand people were in attendance that day, and I could feel the resistance in the room as I spoke out against their witchcraft and diabolic rituals. Their eyes were cold and dark, and many crossed their arms and stared at the floor as I spoke. But God's Spirit was strong within me, and I pressed on with even greater boldness. I didn't hold anything back. I told them about my upbringing, about my parents' satanic beliefs and traditions, and the strong hold that Lucifer had on our family. I told of the hate and abuse he caused in our midst. I testified about the day Jesus came in and set me free, how he broke the curse that Satan had placed on me, and how he later delivered my parents and most of my siblings from this curse as well.

As I exposed Satan and his methods, I could feel the room fill with God's presence. Walls of resistance began coming down. When I gave the altar call, people began flooding into the aisles and racing to the front. I'd never seen so many people running down the middle of a church, crying out in repentance.

All over the sanctuary, big muscular Puerto Rican men were bringing their families forward with tears streaming down their cheeks. Many of the saints in the church came forward to help me pray for all the people coming to receive Christ. As I continued to call for repentance, I could feel the transference of the Spirit of Christ into the souls of lost people as Christians all over the room laid hands on these families and prayed with them. It was a beautiful sight to behold.

Suddenly, about thirty minutes into the invitation, a thought hit me: *My family is going to be attacked!* I hadn't told Gloria and my children that I was going to be speaking against witchcraft, and I knew they wouldn't be prepared for Satan's assault on them. Silently I prayed for God to protect them, then continued ministering to the people in front of me.

It was 1:30 in the morning before the volunteers dropped me off at the front of my hotel. I was physically and spiritually exhausted and couldn't wait to get into bed. I stepped into the elevator, pushed the button to my floor, and watched the door close in front of me.

Suddenly, a clear and discernible voice spoke to me in my spirit, a voice I knew well: *Nicky, your family is under attack but don't be worried. Everything is under control. I promise no harm will come to them. In ten minutes your wife is going to call you. Tell her what she needs to do.*

NO LONGER AFRAID

When I got to my room I took a quick shower and was brushing my teeth when the phone rang. As soon as I answered, I said, "Gloria, I know why you're calling. You're under attack from Satan. Tell me what's happening."

She seemed surprised by my response but frantically began talking. "I was sleeping when the door to my room came open! I went downstairs and started walking around and started hearing all the doors open—every door in the house, including the front and back doors! I even heard the garage door opening! Nicky, what's happening?"

I couldn't remember the last time I had heard Gloria this frightened.

"Calm down, Gloria. Nothing is going to happen to you. I was speaking against Satan tonight, and now he's attacking you. Here's what I want you to do. Go downstairs and make sure all the doors are closed. Then go to the children's rooms and lay your hands on them and pray. Pray for the blood of Jesus to protect our home. Speak aloud to Satan. Tell him he cannot touch us because we are a blessed family. We're the property of Jesus Christ, and nothing can come between us. Command the spirits to leave in the name of Jesus!"

Even as I spoke I could hear Gloria begin to pray. I stayed on the line as she went through the house taking control back from the manifestations of evil that had penetrated our home. And I began to pray while I waited. I prayed that God would build a wall of holy fire around our home to protect my family and that he would send an army of angels to stand against this demonic attack infiltrating our house and frightening my family.

After a while she came back to the phone and told me of the immediate feeling of peace and relief that had come over her and the children. They were no longer afraid.

"Now go back to bed and get some sleep," I told her. "God is in control. Nothing can touch you now!"

CHAPTER SIXTEEN

HOW the ENEMY WORKS

Though I honestly hate giving even an ounce of print to Satan and his ways, it's important that we try to understand the enemy as we follow our Lord's leading in his path toward victory. We need to know how the enemy tries to thwart God's efforts among us.

And nowhere has Satan worked harder at this (or gained greater success) than in his attempts to tear down the family unit.

THE HATRED IS REAL

Satan's hatred toward followers of Christ is very real. He despises all that is good and lovely, everything God stands for, and he'll do all he can to keep people away from the truth. I've witnessed his anger since I was a small child in Puerto Rico. My parents were known throughout the region for their practice of the occult, so I grew up seeing the powerful hold Satan has on those who are under his influence. When my mother became a Christian, it was a fatal blow to the work Satan had built within my family. She was once one of his greatest allies, and now she'd become his fierce enemy.

Just a few months after my mother had given her life to Jesus, Gloria and I were staying at her home. Every night while we were there, at exactly three o'clock in the morning, Gloria would be awakened by a frightening sound outside her window. She said it was a loud, scraping sound, like a fingernail running along the wires of the window screen of our bedroom. I'm a sound sleeper and it never woke me up, but Gloria was getting more afraid each night.

When she told us about it at breakfast one morning, my mother laughed and said, "Don't let that bother you. Ever since I became a Christian the demons have been angry with me. They know they can't have me, but they still try to frighten me. Just ignore it and it will go away. Tell them to shut up, then go back to sleep. After a while they'll stop coming around."

I could tell Gloria wasn't sure what to think of her advice. She didn't grow up seeing the things my family had experienced. But that's how I've always tried to deal with Satan and his wily demons. In spite of their attacks, as frightening as they may seem, the best approach is to simply ignore them and instead focus on the person and power of Jesus. All Satan is trying to do is keep our minds and hearts occupied, to create a diversion in our lives to keep us from telling people about Jesus. The best way to fight him is to disregard his petty antics and continue loving and leading people to salvation. If he had any power over believers, he would have killed all of us long ago.

Paul reminded us that Jesus "disarmed the powers and authorities" and "made a public spectacle of them, triumphing over them by the cross" (Colossians 2:15). Through this act, Jesus gave each of his followers the ability to defuse evil whenever it arises in our presence.

BUG ON A WINDSHIELD

Because of what I do—my direct assaults on Satan's turf—my family has felt his wrath more than most. Gloria and I have always known that our children were targets of his anger, and we've spent many hours of our marriage praying a hedge of protection around our home. God has always been faithful to those requests. But because of Satan's attacks, our children have grown up with a healthy understanding of the Evil One's presence.

Many times my children would come to me with stories of demonic attacks that they'd experienced. I often worried when they were young about how these manifestations might affect them, but as they grew older, it became a natural part of life in our household. They began to understand how weak and powerless evil is in the presence of God's Spirit.

My daughter Nicole once came to me wondering why her friends weren't experiencing the same types of attacks. "When I tell people of the things that happen to me, I get the feeling they don't believe me," she said. "They think I'm exaggerating or making these things up."

I would tell her that I knew how she felt, because people often think the same of me. I explained to her again how Satan is frustrated because all he can do is taunt and frighten, but he can't harm her.

"Satan is nothing more than an annoyance, like a tiny bug on a windshield," I would say. "Just ignore him and go on. He can't do a thing to you."

Still, I understood that to a child his taunting was real and very frightening. And the more effective my ministry became, the greater and more frequent his attacks appeared to be.

A NIGHT OF WARFARE

Once, several years ago, I was holding a crusade in Santa Fe, New Mexico. My family had always noticed that Satan's assaults seemed more profound and aggressive when I ministered in certain places—such as France, Amsterdam, Las Vegas, New York, and certain regions of Latin America—where Satan has a strong foothold and large numbers of people are practicing witchcraft and the occult. Santa Fe has always been one of those places.

During the first night of our crusade, Satan's demons were out in full force taunting my wife and four daughters. They told me later of their experiences.

Nicole was staying at a friend's house that evening. In the middle of the night she woke up and sensed a strange and evil presence in the room. The room was dark, and she couldn't see anything, but she knew something wasn't right. As she peeked out from beneath the covers, she noticed two objects hovering in the corner, several feet away.

She kept her eyes on the figures, hoping they were just her imagination. But they began moving toward her. She closed her eyes tightly, then opened them again to see these two entities staring down at her from the side of the bed. She said she knew instantly what they were, and instinctively began praying and rebuking these evil spirits, commanding them aloud to leave in the name of Jesus. Within a few minutes they were gone.

Alicia, my oldest daughter, was married with one child at the time. During this same night she had a similar experience. She'd been awakened in the middle of the night and felt a strange presence in her home. She was sure she heard noises from other parts of the house. She lay in bed praying and rebuking Satan. Before long the sense of evil subsided.

Gloria was at home with my two other daughters that night, and they experienced attacks of their own. She, too, was awakened in the middle of the night by a strong presence of evil and heard strange noises in her room. She began praying and rebuking the evil spirits. She spent most of that night interceding on behalf of her home and her children. Over breakfast, my other two daughters, Laura and Elena, relayed similar feelings of an evil presence in the home. They, too, had been up much of the night praying.

My entire family spent that night in spiritual warfare, warding off Satan's attacks as I ministered on his turf in Santa Fe. It was a clear indication that he felt threatened by my efforts to bring God's grace to his occultist followers.

I've often worried for my family because of these manifestations of evil. I wondered how these frightening experiences might be affecting their lives and their future. I was glad they were able to see the authority of God over the presence of evil, but I still didn't like that they spent many nights in fear.

Thankfully, God answered the daily prayers Gloria and I lifted up on their behalf, and he used these experiences to instill within my children a deep faith in God and a compassion for helping those blinded by evil. Today all four of my daughters and their husbands are powerful forces for Jesus, and I couldn't be prouder of them.

UNVEILING A DARK PAST

My daughter Nicole is now a practicing psychologist in California. At her place of work she's known as one of the most caring and well-respected therapists in the office. She has been gifted with an amazing insight into human character, and her experiences as a child served only to heighten her awareness of good and evil in the world. Because of her faith, she's able to discern people's hearts and souls as well as their heads. Because of this, she's been wildly successful at helping people overcome their psychological and emotional problems.

Years ago, while she was working toward her degree, she came to me for help with a term paper she'd been assigned. Several of her professors had read or heard of my story, and they were constantly questioning her about me. Nicole became something of a novelty in their department, and they asked her to prepare a research paper on the effects of the occult and witchcraft on society, knowing she would use my past and background as a resource.

"Tell me about my grandparents," Nicole asked me. "I want to write about some of the things you experienced growing up in their home. I've heard a lot of your stories, but tell me what it was really like."

I quickly sensed she was quite serious about wanting to know. Though our kids had spent most of their lives hearing me speak about my past and my testimony, there were parts of my memory that I'd purposely kept from them. Gloria and I had always wanted them to focus more on their own futures and not be burdened with the evil of my past.

Nicole, in particular, had always been fascinated by her roots. I knew that there would come a day when she would want to know everything.

That night I spoke with Gloria about it, and we decided that Nicole was mature enough to handle these dark parts of my past, so the next day we sat down together at the dining room table.

"Are you sure you're ready for this?" I asked her. She assured me she was.

"This is not easy for me," I said. "What I experienced as a child is not pretty, and it's painful for me to remember. But if this will help you with your paper, I'll do it. I'm going to be completely honest with you. If you find this too hard to take, tell me and I'll stop."

She took out a tape recorder and a large yellow pad, and I began.

The Question I Hoped For

For several hours Nicole sat and listened to the stories of my past, including experiences I'd never told in public—tales of witchcraft and sorcery, of satanic possession and spiritual battles, of the abuse and neglect and beatings I endured under the care of my parents.

I told her how I had heard my mother speaking in foreign languages while under the demonic possession of Satan. She spoke languages she couldn't have known—Chinese, Russian, German, and English. I told her of the many times she summoned evil spirits through séances, how she divined people's futures through reading palms, tarot cards, and tea leaves, how she was able to accurately predict deaths and other happenings. When my brother was fighting in the Korean War, my mother went into a trance and in her mind's eye saw his being shot long before we were notified of his near-fatal wounding. She described it to us exactly as it happened, at the moment it was happening.

I told her of the many times my parents had beaten and neglected me, and how my mother used to call me a child of the devil.

Nicole sat stunned, her eyes wide as saucers. "I've always known you had a rough childhood," she told me, "but I had no idea how horrible it really was. I feel so sad for you. For the first time in my life I really appreciate what you must have gone through, how hard it must have been for you to overcome it."

I smiled and took her hand in mine. "It wasn't me, Nicole. It was Jesus. I could have never come through it on my own."

We talked a bit more about my past. Suddenly a thought hit her. "Should we be worried?" she asked. "If Satan had such a strong hold on your family, is he always going to come after us?"

In the back of my mind I was hoping she would ask that question. I leaned back in my chair. "Of course not, sweetie. Jesus has broken the curse! Satan can't touch us anymore. He bugs us and tries to harass us because I hurt him so much, but he has no hold on our family. We are children of God! When I became a Christian, the curse was broken, and it always will be! Don't ever think you'll be punished for my sins or the sins of my family. You belong to Jesus!"

We spent the rest of that evening laughing and joking and praying together. Though I was apprehensive about sharing my past with my little girl, it became something of a freeing and bonding experience for both of us. She did well on her paper, and I was finally able to share some dark parts of my past with one of my five favorite people in the world. It was a therapeutic experience.

CHAPTER SEVENTEEN

The Battle for the Family

Because of my past, nothing grieves my spirit more than to see people living under the curse of Satan. In my travels around the country and the world, I see families everywhere in bondage to the devil. They go through life day after day looking for joy and happiness but never finding it. Fathers and mothers are trying desperately to keep their children from straying, but they feel helpless against the pull of society. Their families are falling apart, and they don't know what to do about it. Most don't even recognize the fact that the source of their helplessness is Satan and the only cure is Jesus.

LETTING OUR GUARD DOWN

So many parents today have let their guards down. They were so anxious to be friends with their kids, to be seen as "cool" and trendy, that they forgot to be parents. They allowed their kids to grow up too quickly and weren't there to guide them and teach them right from wrong. In an effort to give their children material goods, fathers worked harder and longer hours. Mothers flocked to the workplace during a time when their children needed them most. Kids were left to fend for themselves, and today we're experiencing the consequences of our misguided decisions.

More than thirty years ago I began warning people and churches that if we didn't address the drug and violence problem in the inner city, it would soon move to the middle-class and wealthy suburbs. It was obvious then that the real cause of this addictive and destructive behavior was not poverty, but the breakdown of the family unit. At the time, a large percentage of inner-city kids were living in one-parent homes, often lacking male role models. Kids were hungry for guidance, and when they couldn't find it at home they looked to the streets.

This breakdown in the family has now manifested itself in suburban areas, and as a result, drugs, violence, and illicit sexual activity is no longer an inner-city problem but a national one. Today, far more kids in our communities everywhere are from broken homes, and even those living with both their parents are seeing far less of them, as both parents hold down full-time jobs.

Every week I receive letters from young men and women around the country pleading for help. "I can't talk to my parents," they write. "They don't understand. No one understands what I'm going through, the things I'm feeling! I don't know where else to turn!" We're receiving more such letters with each passing year, and their tone is frightening. Most of these cries are coming not from the inner city but from white kids in middle-class and wealthy Christian homes. Many are from the children of pastors and ministers.

Whether we want to admit it or not, we're losing the battle for our children's souls. And until the body of Christ wakes up to this truth and calls on Jesus to help, we'll only decline further into this pit of despair.

FIGHT FOR THEIR SOULS

In spite of how it might sound, my intention is not to make parents feel guiltier than they already do. Over the years I've talked to so many mothers and fathers who feel lost and helpless, wondering where they went wrong and how to go about fixing it. Often they put the blame for their children's way-wardness completely on themselves. They see the ways they've failed their children, and they urgently desire to make it right. But they don't know how.

If this describes where you and your family are at the moment, my advice is to begin by forgiving yourself and your children for the past. Pray a prayer of repentance, then look instead to the future. Hold your head up and take charge, fight back, regain control of your life and your family. Don't let your past define your future.

When we dwell on the negative, it only serves to speak more curses on our family. Instead speak blessings on your children. Say to them, "I know I've made mistakes, and I'm sorry for that. But I'm not going to give up. I'm going to stand with Jesus and see our family through this trying time. I will not allow Satan to manipulate our relationship anymore. Whatever you need, I'm here for you. I will never forsake you. God's beautiful blessings are right in front of you, and I'm going to see that you take them! I'm going to fight for your soul and win!"

THERE'S AN ANSWER

As simplistic as it may sound, there's a solution to putting an end once and for all to gangs and crime and violence and hopelessness among teens of all economic and racial backgrounds. There's a way to fight back. And it begins at home—with you and me—through rebuilding and rediscovering the family unit and putting Christ firmly in place as our foundation.

In spite of what the media and society want us to believe, the only true defense against the ills of our culture is a strong family—a mother and father laboring together, doing the hard work of being good parents to their children. The reason our society is in such disarray is because families have become weakened and fragmented, and the only way to heal our land is to bring families back together.

Today's families—Christian and non-Christian—are under enormous pressure to conform to society's views. Both parents and children are struggling beneath the strain of a world gone mad with sin and temptation. At times it seems we're in a war so one-sided we'll never come out alive. But we must have hope. For the sake of our children we have to hold on, to keep fighting, to stay in the battle, to fight for the integrity of the family—to fight for the souls of our children.

The greatest thing any parent can do for their kids is to lead them into a relationship with Jesus and then mentor them in their faith. Without Jesus, our children are left with no foundation to build on, no measure of right and wrong, no real purpose for their lives. They're forced to look to the world for their value system, and the world always comes up short.

I'm not saying to simply take them to church. I'm talking about introducing them to Jesus—helping them build a relationship with their Lord and Savior. Teach them to love God and his marvelous Word. Bring them face to face with the miracle of the cross—God hanging on a tree, bruised and beaten, blood gushing from his side, innocent and pure, for the sake of our sins! He paid for what we did—and for what we continue to do. His love is deep and real and compassionate. The world doesn't understand this kind of love, but we do! And it's crucial to our children's lives and future that they do as well. Otherwise all the parenting skills in the world won't keep them from straying and falling away from their Lord.

When a family is built on the foundation of Jesus, it instills a sense of hope and purpose. Parents begin to see their children not just as kids to feed and clothe and care for, but as disciples in the faith. They're no longer raising kids; they're mentoring people of God, training them for service in the kingdom as soldiers in a war against spiritual poverty.

When children fall in love with Jesus and allow him to instill in them a sense of passion and purpose, they have no interest in gangs or crime or teen rebellion. They have no time or reason for it. They have a greater mission in life. They begin to focus on others instead of themselves. Their priorities are God's priorities, not those of their peers or their culture. And those priorities create in them a strong sense of worth in the eyes of Jesus and a belief in themselves, their faith, and their calling.

There's an answer to the ills of our culture. There's a way to put an end to violence and hopelessness—not just in the inner city but in every home, school, and neighborhood. We can do it by bringing families back together and introducing them to the power and person of Jesus—by calling on the power of God's Holy Spirit to redeem our past and redefine our future. There is no other answer.

THE CURSE IS BROKEN

Thanks to Jesus, my family and I no longer have to live with the curse of witchcraft that held my parents in bondage for so many years. My children don't have to live with the same evil and chaos that defined my world as a child. When Jesus redeemed my soul, a door opened to my family that allowed God to come in and wipe away Satan's hold on our family's heritage.

That's what the blood of Jesus can do for us. Through the saving grace of Jesus we no longer have to stay bound to the sin of the world. Our lives and our families can overcome the curses of Satan. Through Jesus' obedience at the Cross, humanity was given hope. Families were given a strong foundation to build on. Lost children were given a way out of the hopelessness of sin. Jesus is all we need to begin rebuilding the broken and scarred families of our society and to then keep them strong.

Today I consider myself a blessed man. God gave me the privilege of seeing both my parents come to the Lord before they died, and thirteen of my brothers are now saved. Three of my brothers are ministers of the gospel. And my four precious daughters are all faithful to the Lord and married to wonderful Christian men, two of whom are ministers of the gospel as well. I also have four godly grandchildren to spoil.

In spite of my past, God has blessed me beyond my wildest dreams or imaginations. He has broken the curse.

A few years ago, the night before my beautiful daughter Nicole's wedding, she handed me a letter that brings tears to my eyes every time I read it. I carry it with me wherever I go. She gave me her permission to share it with you. If you're a father, you probably have some sense as to what a love letter like this means to a sentimental old father.

My Sweet Poppy,

Lately it seems there's so much to say to you. Maybe it's because of the changes that are happening, and will be happening in my life. I think of you often. Sometimes I find my mind filled with you.

I think of you walking me down the church aisle and I begin to cry and cry. It will be so hard to release your arm for Rob's and take his name.

There is a big part of me that always wants to be your little girl, reliant on my big dad. That's why it's so important to tell you that I realize now how big you are in my life, how deep my love is for you, how much of myself comes from you.

This will never change. I will always need you, always love you. You will always be my Poppy—only you. There will never be another person that I look into their face and life and see myself and what I might be. Your presence fills my life, more than you realize.

I also want you to know, Dad, that I've seen your best and I've seen your worst, and you will always be my hero, as well as my dad.

I'm afraid to stop writing. I'm afraid that I haven't said enough. It's so important that you know how much I love you. Thank you for being strong. Thank you for staying married to mom. Thank you for being the covering over my life for 29 years—you've done so well. Thank you for providing for us, for giving me so much more than I need.

Thank you for helping me to believe in miracles—we are both miracles.

Thank you for being a fighter—in the good way. Thank you for making God and love the most important. Thank you for serving God faithfully—until the end.

I will carry your name in my name, and more importantly, in my heart.

With a true love, your daughter,

Nicole Cruz

There are no words to describe the feelings of joy and accomplishment that come from knowing that your family is rooted firmly in the tree of life—that you've fought for the souls of your children and won.

I wish that joy on every person and parent within God's earthly kingdom.

PART 3

The oneness

I will give them an undivided heart and put a new spirit in them; I will remove from them their heart of stone and give them a heart of flesh. Then they will follow my decrees and be careful to keep my laws. They will be my people, and I will be their God.

EZEKIEL 11:19-20

I pray also for those who will believe in me…that all of them may be one, Father, just as you are in me and I am in you. May they also be in us so that the world may believe that you have sent me.

JOHN 17:20-21

May the God who gives endurance and encouragement give you a spirit of unity among yourselves as you follow Christ Jesus, so that with one heart and mouth you may glorify the God and Father of our Lord Jesus Christ.

ROMANS 15:5-6

There is one body and one Spirit—just as you were called to one hope when you were called—one Lord, one faith, one baptism; one God and Father of all, who is over all and through all and in all.

EPHESIANS 4:4-6

one mission, one message

After the Holy Spirit first gave birth to the church and marked these first followers of Jesus by his holy fire, the immediate results in their lives were dramatic and all-encompassing:

> They devoted themselves to the apostles' teaching and to the fellowship, to the breaking of bread and to prayer. Everyone was filled with awe, and many wonders and miraculous signs were done by the apostles. All the believers were together and had everything in common. Selling their possessions and goods, they gave to anyone as he had need. Every day they continued to meet together in the temple courts. They broke bread in their homes and ate together with glad and sincere hearts, praising God and enjoying the favor of all the people. And the Lord added to their number daily those who were being saved. (Acts 2:42-47)

Call me a dreamer and an idealist, but I long for that kind of church today—a unified body of Christ. And I believe God longs for this as well.

It's a church united by a clear vision of our supreme and compelling mission and purpose in this world.

It's a church drawn together as believers everywhere learn to view the lost people all around them as God sees them.

And it's a church that shares with these lost souls a single, simple, unifying message—the good news of Jesus.

Is this really so hard to imagine?

We've seen how God's Spirit leads and guides his followers to draw people to himself. But what can be accomplished when his people move together in vision and purpose, unified in the mission to reach the lost? How powerfully is God willing to work through the lives of followers who put away their prejudices, ideologies, and personal agendas and unite with one primary goal in mind—to save souls?

What if we bound together as one in our war on pain and hopelessness, beckoning God's Spirit to "comfort us"—to push us forward into battle and to release his power within us?

The first-century believers took that challenge, and God used their faithfulness to make an eternal impact on their culture and the world. They began in a small room with a handful of people. But what would happen today if God's people—who now number in the hundreds of millions worldwide—accepted that same call? What if we decided today to put away our preconceptions about God and the Holy Spirit, to come together as one unit and one body, and to simply do as they did—believe in God's power and trust him to lead?

THESE ARE MY PEOPLE

When I move through the lonely sidewalks of an inner-city neighborhood, the memories of my past come flooding back into my mind. I can taste the oppression, the hopelessness. I smell the fragrance of sin and death and hate. I hear the sounds of bondage, the chains of poverty and addiction. I feel the anguish. Once again I am transported back to my days on the streets of New York when I, too, was lost and helpless, yearning for relief from my misery. I never want to forget the life that Jesus took me out of.

And what I see on the streets are faces of emptiness, people longing for help, people searching for something more. People who need Jesus. This is where I see it most clearly because it's the life God saved me from. These are my people. I relate to them. The bond we share is real and profound. That's why God called me to this mission field—because my past is so interconnected with their present.

But you don't have to go to the inner city to find hopelessness. The poor have no monopoly on sin and despair. It's just as easy to see the faces of emptiness in a mansion in L.A., in a New York high-rise, or in a Midwestern farmhouse. Satan has set up shop in homes and neighborhoods in every corner of the planet. I am called to minister to the inner city, but God's purpose for you may be to simply reach out in your school or workplace, or on the street where you live. If you want to find your calling, look at where God has placed you, at the people he has put in your life, and at your family. That's your ministry—your responsibility before God.

You and I may not have the same mission field, but we share the same mission—to evangelize the world. That's what we're here for. This is Jesus' command to us all.

WHY WE'RE ON THIS PLANET

"I have come down from heaven," Jesus once said, "not to do my will but to do the will of him who sent me. And this is the will of him who sent me, that I shall lose none of all that he has given me, but raise them up at the last day. For my Father's will is that everyone who looks to the Son and believes in him shall have eternal life, and I will raise him up at the last day" (John 6:38-40).

Jesus understood his purpose on earth—to save the world and bring sinners back to God. It was the passion of his heart—his one and only vision.

Throughout his entire time on earth, Jesus had but one important appointment to keep—the Cross and all that it required. He never lost sight of God's vision for his ministry. It gave him a crystal-clear focus in all that he said and did, and because of it people were drawn to him. He knew where he came from and where he was going. His authority and confidence came from God.

You and I need that same kind of vision and purpose in our lives. We need to discover what God has put us on this planet to accomplish—our gifts, our ministry, our role in the body of Christ, our mission field. If we want God to use us to draw people to himself, we need to first understand his primary intent for us within his greater plan.

I was just twenty-two when God imparted into my heart his will for me to become an evangelist. He instructed me to use my past and my testimony to draw sinners to salvation, and since that time I've remained faithful to that calling. At times I've grown tired of telling my story, and I've wished God would use me for another purpose. It's hard to relive the memories over and over again in my mind.

Often I've thought to myself, *What harm would it be if I simply went into another line of ministry? Maybe I could pastor a church or put together a seminar on marriage-and-family issues—something that would allow me to use more of my gifts and talents? Or maybe I could go into business? I'm sure I could do well as an entrepreneur. It would certainly pay better!*

But then I remember my calling, and those thoughts quickly subside. There's nothing wrong with any of these professions; they're simply not what God intended for my life. I'm an evangelist, an ambassador of God's grace and forgiveness. I tell people about Jesus and lead them to salvation before his throne. That is my purpose before God as well as my spiritual gift. When God called me to that profession, he not only gave me the ability to carry it out, but he placed in my heart a compassion for the lost. He gave me eyes to see clearly the people who need forgiveness, then he set me on a path to find them. And because I've tried to stay true to that vision, he's been able to use me for his glory. Gloria has always felt this same call on her life, and today we're blessed to have two daughters and their husbands working in full-time ministry.

You may have another calling and profession. God has created each of us with different talents and gifts, with different purposes in mind for us. But still, all of us are called to reach the lost, and we're each given talents toward that end. It's our job to clearly discern our role in furthering God's kingdom on earth, to seek out his direction and vision for our lives, and to stay on course. Once we discover our purpose in God's greater plan, we need to remain focused and committed to that cause.

OUR COMPELLING OFFER

As Jesus ministered to the Samaritan woman at the well, he offered her something she could get nowhere else—"living water." He said to her, "Everyone who drinks this [physical] water will be thirsty again, but whoever drinks the water I give him will never thirst. Indeed, the water I give him will become in him a spring of water welling up to eternal life" (John 4:13-14).

What he promised the woman was hope, a way out of the despair and helplessness of a life embedded in sin. It was the one thing she most needed.

Thanks to Jesus' obedience at the Cross, we have the ability to make that same offer to everyone we meet. Our message is one of hope and forgiveness and freedom, a message people can get nowhere else but at the feet of Jesus. We hold in our hands the only satisfying drink of water in the middle of a dry and unrelenting desert, and all around us are people dying of thirst. All we need to do is reach out and make the offer, and Jesus will do the rest.

It's important to remember, however, that a message of love and forgiveness needs to be presented with great compassion. Too often we present the gospel the way that Peter responded to the soldiers who came to take Jesus at Gethsemane (John 18:10)—by raising a sword and cutting off someone's ear. (It's hard to hear the good news when your ear is lying on the ground!)

Just a few months ago my daughter Nicole and her husband, Rob, were attending the Tournament of Roses Parade in Pasadena. They were strolling through the huge crowds gathered on the streets, enjoying the festivities and awaiting the start of the parade.

Suddenly, a truck came barreling down Colorado Boulevard. It was plastered with signs and Scripture references on every side. ACCEPT JESUS OR DIE! one sign read. On another was a picture of fire, accompanied by some words that they couldn't quite make out. The driver was an unkempt, middle-aged man with a megaphone pressed to his lips and aimed out the window. "Repent sinners!" he screamed. "If you don't know Jesus, you're going to burn in hell!"

As the man turned the corner, people in the crowd started yelling obscenities and throwing rocks and trash at his truck. Several raised their fists in anger as the man sped down the road. Rob and Nicole overheard the angry bystanders talking among themselves. "What a jerk," said one person. "That's why I'll never become a Christian," said another, "because they're all just hateful weirdos!"

I shudder to think about how much the cause of Christ was set back that evening, thanks to this angry, misguided believer. Though his passion for preaching salvation may have been well intentioned, his method was pathetic.

WHATEVER IT TAKES

If we want to reach people for Jesus, let's instead take a lesson from the apostle Paul when he was speaking in Athens. He knew how to reach people with the message of salvation.

While there in Athens, waiting for his friends Silas and Timothy, Paul became distressed over the huge number of people worshiping idols and false gods. He was repulsed and angered by these practices, wanting to rebuke and correct the Athenians for their evil ways. But he knew how deeply embedded these rituals were in their culture, so he weighed his words carefully. He knew that in order to reach them, he needed to first gain their trust, so he spent some time in the city getting to know the people and their culture. He talked with the people on the streets and learned about their values and beliefs. He ate what they ate and wore what they wore. He learned what was important to them, what they talked about, what they feared, who they worshiped. He read their books and listened to their poetry. He got inside their heads and their hearts.

Paul was living out the very philosophy of evangelism that he wrote about in his letter to the church at Corinth: "I have become all things to all men so that by all possible means I might save some" (1 Corinthians 9:22).

That's exactly what he was doing during his stay in Athens—learning to become one of them so he could better relay God's message of hope.

When a group of Epicurean and Stoic philosophers heard him preaching about Jesus on the streets and in the synagogue, they took him to a meeting of the Areopagus to argue with him. They were armed and ready for a fight—and on their own turf. Paul wisely laid aside his hostility and used the Athenians' hunger for spiritual knowledge to his favor. Surrounded by the sculptured images of the many gods they worshiped, he began by commending them for their interest in seeking the truth:

Men of Athens! I see that in every way you are very religious. For as I walked around and looked carefully at your objects of worship, I even found an altar with this inscription: TO AN UNKNOWN GOD. Now what you worship as something unknown I am going to proclaim to you. (Acts 17:22-23)

Instead of insulting their intelligence, he used their hunger for knowledge to his advantage. He complimented them on their diligent searching, and when he had their attention, he shared the truth of Jesus. He spoke to them with eloquence and ease, using the type of poetic language they were known for. It was one of the most brilliant examples of effective evangelism ever recorded. Through his tactful approach, Paul was able to break down the barriers and reach many hardened people for Christ.

One of the reasons our ministry to the inner city has been so effective in reaching the lost is that we've always been committed to this same approach. I'll do whatever it takes to reach people with the gospel.

Our use of rap and hip-hop music in our outreach concerts, as I mentioned earlier, is one good example of this. Years ago, rap began in the ghetto as a cry for help. Kids were looking for a way to vent their anger, to release their pain, to let people know of the loneliness and fear that surrounded their streets and defined their world. They wanted a way out. And when help didn't come, their lyrics turned more violent and angry. Instead of venting their helplessness, they were now screaming out in rage against authority and the society that they felt had let them down. The gangs took rap music to another level, encouraging violence and wrath against policemen and other gangs.

When we began using rap as a means of preaching the gospel, we came under a lot of criticism and fire from the Christian community. We had a hard time convincing people we were simply trying to take one of the devil's tools of sin and use it for God's glory. In spite of the criticism, we knew we were on the right track, so we persisted. Today, rap music has become one of the best tools we've found for breaking down the barriers of resentment and introducing people to Jesus.

If you want to reach people with the gospel, you have to be willing to speak their language, to get inside their heads and their hearts, to become "all things to all people."

Our world has too many followers who point their rigid fingers at sinners in condemnation. What we need are more Christians who are willing to show love and respect and kindness to the lost and searching. God needs people who are willing to hold and embrace sinners and gently guide them to the truth of his word—compassionate hearts with a compelling message.

seeing people as god sees them

Some people who had heard of the miracles Jesus was performing once brought a blind man to him. Jesus could have healed the man in front of his friends, but instead he chose to take him by the hand and lead him to a secluded place outside the village. When they were alone, he spat in the man's eyes. In any culture this would be considered an insult. It's like asking a bald man to let down his hair—something you just don't do in a polite society. But Jesus did it anyway.

Jesus then asked the man if he could see anything, and he answered, "I see people; they look like trees walking around."

I'm sure the man was thrilled to have even a hint of sight, but Jesus wanted the man to see clearly, to know what he'd been missing, to witness the full glory of his Father's creation. So he put his hands over the man's eyes again, and suddenly the man could see clearly. His sight was completely restored (Mark 8:22-25).

OUR BLURRY VISION

In so many ways I've seen God do the same thing in my life. When I first gave my heart to him, I could see for the first time. It was a glorious feeling. But my vision was blurry and confusing and new. Through the years he continued to disciple me, to shape my heart and spirit, to place his hands over my eyes until I could see more clearly. I began to see people plainly, as individuals before me, not as simple masses moving about. I began to see them the way *he* sees them—hurting and lost, like sheep without a shepherd.

That's what Jesus' touch on our lives will do for us, but only if we're willing to let him. So many followers of Christ never get to that stage. We allow God to touch us, to set us free from the blindness, the total darkness of sin, but we somehow remain content with an immature sight. We see people as trees walking around, as fuzzy images before us, but we never allow Jesus to touch us deeper, to bring our eyes and hearts into clear focus. We don't allow him to take us further into the vision he has in mind for us, to help us see people the way he sees them.

Where so many of us see vague masses moving to and fro before us, God sees faces of anguish, individual souls wandering aimlessly through life and desperately seeking freedom from their pain. As he looks closer he sees the scars and bruises, the wounds of a life enslaved to sin. Their hearts are cold and broken. Their wounds are deep. Their tears are real.

Once we see people this way—as individuals in search of freedom from their pain—we begin to feel for them. We develop a deep compassion and a desire to help. We begin to see people through God's eyes, as lost and miserable souls desperately in need of a Savior.

If there's one message I want every believer to take away from this book, it's this: *Open your eyes to the lost and hopeless around you. Allow the Holy Spirit to let you see them the way God sees them.*

And once our eyes are truly open in this way, our lives are never again the same. When we see people the way God sees them, when we feel for them as he feels for them, it creates within us a wave of love and compassion for the lost. We begin to hurt for them, to weep for them, to lose sleep over the thought of their losing their souls to Satan. And we begin to pray earnestly for the Holy Spirit to guide our words and convict their spirits as we try to reach them.

HOW WE TREAT TODAY'S LEPERS

Time and again the Gospels portray Jesus as a man of deep and unwavering compassion. After the death of John the Baptist, Jesus withdrew alone on a boat to mourn the loss of his friend and cousin. He knew John was in heaven, but he hurt for those who were left behind. His tears were real.

When Jesus returned to shore, he saw a crowd of five thousand people gathered to see him. Matthew records that he "had compassion on them." So he took five loaves of bread and two fish and miraculously provided food for them all (Matthew 14:14-21). His heart went out to these people who had come to be with him, and he couldn't stand to see them hungry. His love was real and genuine, and he acted upon those feelings. He not only provided food, but he also healed the ones who were sick.

When Jesus saw two blind men on the road to Jericho, he "had compassion on them and touched their eyes. Immediately they received their sight and followed him" (Matthew 20:34). Jesus wasn't interested in making a name for himself or proving his power. He simply saw that they had a need and knew that he was able to help them, so he did. His compassion for these men outweighed any other task before him at the moment.

On the road between Samaria and Galilee, while going into a small village, Jesus noticed ten men who had leprosy. "They stood at a distance and called out in a loud voice, 'Jesus, Master, have pity on us!' When he saw them, he said, 'Go, show yourselves to the priests.' And as they went, they were cleansed" (Luke 17:12-14).

The lepers instinctively kept their distance, even from Jesus. Society had shunned and ignored them. They were unacceptable. Rejected by the world.

They had no names, no addresses, no identities—the scourges of their culture. No one wanted to get near them. Their bodies reeked of disease and filth—the smell of death. They'd been placed out of sight and out of mind by those who didn't want to believe they existed, didn't want to help, didn't want to see their ugly, dirty, dying faces.

But Jesus *saw* them. Though they were far away, he looked in their direction and had compassion on them. He respected them as men—not as diseased and contagious lepers, but as individual people in desperate need of help. People in need of a Savior. And even though only one of the men came back to thank him, all ten of them experienced his healing touch. His compassion was not only real but unconditional.

How do we respond to the lepers of our day—the outcasts of society? What does our culture do with the poor, the addicts, the alcoholics, the gang members, the gays, the AIDS patients, the sinners? More important, what does the body of Christ do with them? Do we see them as people in need of help, lost and searching for a way out of their despair and bondage? Or do we pretend they don't exist? Do we keep them confined, out of sight and out of mind, somewhere far from our eyes, so we don't have to deal with them?

We've forgotten what Jesus has done for us. We've forgotten that without his saving grace we would be just as lost and hopeless and blind as they are. If you took away our nice clothes and fancy cars, our houses and jewelry and jobs, our health and strength and faith, we, too, would be unwanted. Without Jesus we are nothing. And without compassion we have no place in God's kingdom and no right to call ourselves sons and daughters of the King.

Time and again in Scripture we see Jesus going out of his way to touch the life of just one person. Even in the midst of large crowds he often focused on the needs of a poor beggar, a prostitute, a tax collector, a fisherman, a lame or blind man. He didn't see crowds; he saw people. He didn't see fame or glory or praise; he saw only needy souls looking for help.

Imagine the impact we could have on our world if every minister, pastor, evangelist, and believer today saw people that way. If only we could put away our need to draw attention to ourselves and focus instead on the needs before us, the faces of loneliness, the eyes of pain and confusion that sit on every corner of the globe.

THIS IS HOW WE KNOW

When our eyes have been opened by Jesus—when we see people the way he sees them—we can no longer sit quietly while hurting souls wander aimlessly through life all around us. Compassion for the lost cannot coexist with complacency. Apathy is no longer an option.

"This is how we know who the children of God are," the apostle John tells us, "and who the children of the devil are: Anyone who does not do what is right is not a child of God; nor is anyone who *does not love his brother*" (1 John 3:10). Does God's Word get any clearer than this? There's a litmus test to see if we're true followers of Jesus, to see if we're really his children, and it hinges on the level of our compassion for others.

John goes on to write,

> If anyone has material possessions and sees his brother in need but
> has no pity on him, *how can the love of God be in him?* Dear children,
> let us not love with words or tongue but with actions and in truth.
> This then is how we know that we belong to the truth, and how we
> set our hearts at rest in his presence whenever our hearts condemn us.
> (1 John 3:17-20)

When the Holy Spirit has come into our hearts and lives, filling us with the love and compassion of Jesus, we see people clearly. Our eyes shine with the joy of the Lord, and we can no longer walk by a leper without seeing him, without feeling his pain. We take it upon ourselves to help him restore his dignity before God. We embrace him, cry with him, and lead him into the healing arms of Jesus. That's what being a follower of Christ is all about.

coming together—
to spend ourselves

Here's a dilemma I've never been able to understand: As I travel around the country, speaking at crusades and outreaches around the world, I have the opportunity to meet and interact with a lot of churches and pastors. I hear stories of frustration in the ministry. Pastors everywhere are wondering why their churches aren't growing, often becoming disillusioned themselves and stepping down and going into the work force. Seminaries are enrolling fewer ministerial students each year. Because of these facts, there's a serious shortage of pastors in this country today, and churches are dying out, losing more and more of their members to large megachurches, where people often get lost in the crowd.

At the same time, I regularly witness huge numbers of people coming to the Lord at our hit-and-run outreaches and our *Run Baby Run* crusades. Every time we target a city for a four-month evangelistic crusade, we reach thousands of inner-city kids with the gospel. The churches that partner with us in these efforts struggle to keep up with the names and faces of all the new converts, and I'm continually bothered at the thought of how many of these souls are slipping through the cracks, simply because of our lack of manpower.

WHY THE INNER CITY EXISTS

I'm not naive—I know why most churches aren't interested in growing through inner-city outreach. Poor people with violent upbringings don't have a lot to offer a church, especially one in the suburbs. They bring with them a lot of baggage and very little money. They're a needy group—financially, emotionally, and spiritually. It's easier to simply let another church deal with them, perhaps one in the inner city that's used to addressing their types of problems.

Poor ghetto neighborhoods seldom show up on most churches' target demographic sheets. That doesn't surprise me, but it does burden my heart deeply.

In fact, if we were truly honest about it, we would admit that the only reason there *is* an inner city—this clear geographical chasm between the haves and the have-nots—is because *the church has allowed it to happen.* We've sat on our hands and turned a deaf ear to the suffering and plight of the poor, expecting the government to take care of them. When their efforts don't work, we shake our heads, complain about public policy, and lock our doors even tighter. But it isn't the government that has failed them, it's the church—you and me—the followers of Christ. President George W. Bush has often espoused those same thoughts, and I couldn't agree more with him.

AWAY WITH THE YOKE

God has clearly voiced his feelings on this issue throughout Scripture over and over again. Through the prophet Isaiah, God cried out to the nation of Israel, condemning them for their apathy toward the poor.

> *Is not this the kind of fasting I have chosen:*
> *to loose the chains of injustice*
> *and untie the cords of the yoke,*

to set the oppressed free
and break every yoke?
Is it not to share your food with the hungry
and to provide the poor wanderer with shelter—
when you see the naked, to clothe him,
and not to turn away from your own flesh and blood?...

If you do away with the yoke of oppression,
with the pointing finger and malicious talk,
and if you spend yourselves in behalf of the hungry
and satisfy the needs of the oppressed,
then your light will rise in the darkness. (Isaiah 58:6-7,9-10)

If God's people today—the body of Christ from all denominations— came together as one unit with the single purpose to "do away with the yoke of oppression" and adopt an unwavering commitment to "spend" ourselves on behalf of the hungry, not only would we see a wave of healing pour across our land, breaking down the racial and economic barriers that separate the poor and the rich, but our churches would be overflowing. We wouldn't be able to build auditoriums fast enough to hold all the people coming to Christ.

All this can happen simply through our obedience to God's commands regarding the poor and downtrodden.

A HOPELESS SITUATION

A few years ago God gave me a foreshadowing glimpse into this possibility during one of our most powerful TRUCE crusades, which occurred in Milwaukee.

During the planning stages of our outreach, we identified a prominent Christian leader in the area whom we hoped to bring on as a chairperson. This man was well networked within the community and had ties to many city officials, church and business leaders, local politicians, and media people. His connections would have proven valuable in our efforts for physical and financial support from the community. I sent one of our ministry workers on a preliminary visit with this man to gauge his interest. He took a TRUCE worker with him, an ex-thug from Philadelphia who had been led to Christ by my good friend Reggie White.

Milwaukee was well known for its no-nonsense approach to crime and its lack of compassion for the inner city. The mayor was a hard but fair man who had been very vocal about his antigang, zero-tolerance policy on drugs and gang activity. As he disdained the violence and crime in the inner city, he showed little tolerance for criminals. His stance was popular with the people, yet in spite of his policies on crime, the problem wasn't going away. Poverty and gang crime continued to rise to near epidemic proportions.

Businesses were afraid of the inner city and wouldn't put their plants and factories anywhere near it. The economy was growing but moving to the outskirts of the city. Suburban areas were moving outward as well, and middle-class people never ventured into the poorer areas. So the inner city continued to grow—both in size and population. This dynamic is a common one among large cities in the United States, but in Milwaukee the problem seemed even greater and more pronounced.

In the middle of this seemingly hopeless situation, our two ambassadors found themselves sitting across the table from this prominent city leader, trying to convince him to help in our efforts to reach out to the poor urban areas.

They explained our intentions in detail, outlining our plans for a series of hit-and-run outreaches culminating in a nine-day performance of our *Run Baby Run* production at a local college auditorium. The two shared stories of our past successes in other major cities. The man listened intently, waiting for them to finish, then leaned back in his chair to contemplate his response.

Finally, he said, "It sounds like a good idea on the surface, and I'd like to think it would work, but I can tell you it won't. Not here, anyway. No one's interested in helping the inner city. Sure, they need the gospel, but what's going to happen after we save them? What are they going to do then? Where are we going to put them? Who's going to take care of them? Our churches aren't equipped to deal with their problems, and they're just going to end up back on the streets in the same shape they were in before. What difference are we really going to make? I'd really like to help, but I honestly think your time would be better spent reaching out in another city."

Our TRUCE workers sat stunned. For the first time they understood what an uphill battle it would be to mobilize this hardened city for help.

After letting his words sink in, the man turned to the ex-thug and asked, "Tell me what you think. What would it take for a crusade to work in this city?"

The young man thought for a minute, then said, "What I think is, this city needs more people like Nicky Cruz and his TRUCE workers. Then you wouldn't have such a big problem in the inner city. You wouldn't have the kind of drugs and killings and gangs that you do. In fact, there probably wouldn't even be an inner city and a suburb, just people living together and helping each other when it's needed. Because Nicky treats people with respect."

The man thought long and hard about his words, but in the end he still saw no way that he could convince the city's churches and leaders to help with our crusade. He declined our offer and again encouraged us to move on to a place where our efforts would be better received.

Our two ambassadors came home feeling dejected, and our ministry worker told me of their encounter the next day. "It doesn't look like we're going to get much help from the church leaders," he told me.

I thought about that for a minute then said, "Good. Now I know that God wants us there. He's the only one who can make this happen, and when he does, no one will be able to take the credit. Whatever happens, everyone will have to admit that God is the one who did it, not us!"

We immediately set the matter to prayer and decided to go ahead with our crusade without any help from the city leaders. If God wanted the area churches and Christians to help, he would have to lead them to us.

Over the weeks and months to come, that's exactly what he did.

An Encounter Planned by God

Several weeks later I was invited to a dinner at the home of a prominent businessman in the area. I was there to meet with a wealthy man from Milwaukee who had offered financial support for our ministry and with the pastor of a large, influential Lutheran church in the area. The pastor was asked to bless the meal, but first he turned to me and said, "Mr. Cruz, before I pray I'd like to tell you a story.

"When I was a little boy, my father got saved by watching Billy Graham on television. I remember him putting his hand on the television screen and asking Jesus into his heart. After that he was on fire for the Lord. He went door to door telling people about Jesus.

"One day he took me to a church building to watch a movie called *The Cross and the Switchblade*. I had never seen anything that affected me like that movie did. I couldn't believe what God had done in the life of a young teenager named Nicky Cruz. That night I went up to my mom and said, 'If God can make Nicky Cruz an evangelist, I know he can do the same for me. I know I'm supposed to be a pastor.' I was fourteen at the time, and since that day I've never veered from that belief.

"I've been a pastor now for over twenty-five years, and today I'm finally able to stand face to face with the man who impacted my life like no other. I want to thank you for staying faithful to God. It's truly an honor to have dinner with you tonight."

His words touched me deeply. I'm always grateful to God for bringing about these small confirmations of my ministry—letting me see firsthand the impact my story has had on others. It always warms my heart.

Just before praying, the pastor added, "If there's anything you need, my church and my home are open for you. All you need to do is ask. We're happy to help in any way we can."

I knew then that God had orchestrated this encounter. After dinner I discussed with this pastor the crusade we were planning, and he asked if he and his church could partner with us in our efforts. He also offered to be our local chairperson. At first I wasn't sure what to expect, given the church's doctrinally conservative views—many of our methods are pretty far outside the comfort zones of most Christians—but we trusted that the Lord knew what he was doing.

His was the first congregation in the area to sign on and help us reach Milwaukee's inner city—the first of many pieces to fall into place in this divine puzzle God was working.

EYES OF ANGER

This pastor and I began to develop a good relationship over the coming weeks and months, and he asked me to speak at his church to relay our vision to the congregation. While standing in his pulpit, sharing my message, I noticed a young man sitting near the back of the auditorium. He was tall and lanky, with unkempt brown hair. His eyes looked dark and empty and tired. Even from a distance I could tell he was high on some kind of drug.

During my message I noticed him jump out of his chair and walk quickly out the back door. A man in the seat next to him followed him out and a few minutes later brought him back into the auditorium, abruptly returning him to his seat. The boy sat hunched in his chair with his arms folded across his chest and his feet extended beneath the seat in front of him.

After giving an invitation and praying for the people who had come forward, I made my way back to where the boy was sitting. He seemed embarrassed by the attention.

"I see a lot of anger in your eyes," I told him. "I can tell you don't want to be here. But you need to know that you're here because God brought you here. He's trying to reach you. Why do you resist him?"

The boy sat motionless, staring at the ground in front of him. For a long time he didn't speak. Suddenly he looked up at me, and I could see a tear forming in the corner of his eye.

"I'm going to pray for you now," I said. "I want you to listen to my words and receive them. Jesus wants to forgive you if you'll just ask him to."

As I prayed for the boy, tears ran down his cheeks and onto the carpet beneath us. He couldn't speak; he just cried uncontrollably. I could tell he was hurting, that he was trying to receive Christ, but the pain was still there. He was a boy with a lot of baggage, and his healing would take some time.

After the service I took aside one of my ministry workers, a man named Vaso, and told him to keep an eye on the young man. "I want you to follow him and talk to him," I said. "We need to follow up on this kid. He's so close to giving himself over to God, but he's not there yet."

A few days later, Vaso got a call at his hotel room from the youth pastor of this Lutheran church.

"You remember that young boy that Nicky prayed for last Sunday?" the pastor asked.

"Yes, I know the boy you're talking about," Vaso answered.

"Well, I'm not sure if you know, but he's been living in a house with a bunch of other kids who are hooked on drugs. A drug dealer in the area rents the house, and he lets a lot of runaways stay there. We've been trying to help this boy for a long time, but we really don't know what to do, and neither do his parents. We're not equipped to handle this type of thing, and we were wondering if you might be able to help us. I think Nicky really touched him last Sunday, but we can't help him as long as he's living in this house and doing drugs. Would you talk to him?"

Vaso has never shied away from a good fight with Satan. "I'm going to do better than that," he said. "I'm going to go get him. I'll get some people together, and you and I will go over there and have a talk with these people."

ON SATAN'S TURF

Vaso is an intimidating figure—six feet seven with more than three hundred pounds of bones and muscle—and he seldom has trouble getting someone's attention when he wants it. He also has a deep love for the Lord and a heart for the lost and hurting. He was the perfect person to head up this righteous expedition.

Through connections in our TRUCE ministry, Vaso called on the help of a few inner-city pastors in the area, ones who had developed some experience dealing with drug- and sex-addiction in teens. One was a female urban missionary who had been saved from a life of prostitution and drug abuse on the streets several years earlier.

After Vaso picked up his team and connected with the pastor, they made the forty-five-minute drive to the house in which these kids were staying. After they pulled up to the curb in front of the large suburban house, from the street they could see lights on in most of the windows. But before going to the door, they drove around the corner and spent a half-hour in fervent prayer over their efforts. My workers know the importance of being in the Spirit before trying to minister on Satan's turf.

They drove back to the house and knocked on the door for several minutes, but no one answered. Through a window near the door they could see people moving about inside the house. After a few minutes, they saw a young man approaching from the street behind them. He walked up to the house, stepped past them, and opened the front door. Vaso followed him and said, "We're coming in with you. Is that okay?"

The young man looked up at Vaso's large frame and quickly agreed.

The house was bustling with young kids, many of whom were dressed in black gothic clothing. Most had pierced tongues, noses, and eyebrows. One young girl walked through the hallway wearing a spiked dog collar.

Vaso immediately walked from room to room and commanded everyone to gather in the living room.

"Who are you?" they kept asking.

"Never mind who I am, just get into the living room," he bellowed. "We need to talk."

Within a few minutes, twenty-one people had gathered in the middle of the home's large living area to the left of the front entrance, including the young man I had prayed over at the Lutheran church. Most appeared to be high on drugs, and several looked as though they'd been physically abused. The house was littered with beer cans and wine bottles, and the air reeked of cigarette and marijuana smoke. Drug paraphernalia sat on several end tables. A Satanic bible lay on a couch in one of the lower-level rooms. The team was surprised at how young many of the people seemed.

"I know you people hate Christians," Vaso began. "There was a time not long ago when I did too. You think God doesn't care about you, and you're probably not interested in what we have to say. But we're here to tell you about Jesus. All we want is fifteen minutes of your time, and after that, if you still want us to leave, I give you my word that we will. You can do what you want with our message, but we want you to listen to us first. That's all we're asking. We know Jesus can change your lives forever, but whether or not you let him is up to you. All we want is fifteen minutes, then we'll leave. Fair enough?"

The kids nodded reluctantly.

ARE YOU HAPPY?

Vaso introduced a young woman who had come with the missionary group. He stepped aside as she shared her testimony to the group.

"When I was just a child," she told them, "I was molested by my father and my older brothers. They raped me every chance they got. There was nothing I could do to stop them, so I just took it. When I turned twelve, my mom found out about it and blamed me. She called me a tramp and said it was all my fault. Then she told me, 'Since you're already having sex you might as well get paid for it,' so I became a prostitute. I had a baby when I was fifteen.

"At twenty-one I moved to the city to try to get out of that lifestyle. Instead I got involved with a man who got me hooked on drugs. The only way I could make enough money to support my habit was to go back into the streets as a hooker. Before long I was supporting his habit too. That's what I did for the next several years. I'd leave my daughter home alone while I walked the streets. During those years all I cared about was getting enough money to keep myself high. I didn't care about myself—only the drugs and booze.

"Then one day a pastor took in me and my daughter and helped me dry out. He hid us and kept us safe, and he told me about Jesus. I didn't think anyone cared about me, and I couldn't imagine that God could forgive me. But he did. I gave my heart to Jesus, and he started to love me and change my life."

The kids were visibly moved by this woman's testimony. As she continued to share her story, the walls they'd built began crumbling to the ground. Several could not hold back their tears.

She continued her story: "When I was on drugs, I told everyone I was happy, and I pretended to be having a good time, but I was living in hell. It was miserable." She paused to wipe the tears from her eyes. "The worst part is, I knew I was going to hell. And I didn't want to go to hell!"

As her tears flowed, one of the other pastors stood up and addressed the kids. "Let me ask you a question," he said. "Are you happy? Do you like the life you're living—staying high and hiding from the police? Is this life really what you thought it would be?"

One by one the kids began responding to his challenge for honesty. Several broke down and cried as they shared similar stories of abuse and helplessness. Before long all twenty-one of the people had fallen under the conviction of the Holy Spirit and were asking for help. Vaso and his unlikely team of missionaries wept and prayed with the young people, embracing their pain and bringing them to Christ. It was a powerful evening of victory for the cause of Christ.

A CHURCH BEGINS TO CHANGE

What happened over the next few weeks and months was nothing short of miraculous. The youth pastor of the Lutheran church began ministering to and mentoring these twenty-one new converts. Some of the runaway children were reunited with their families, and others from the home were accepted and loved by the congregation. The church members took them into their homes and helped them dry out from their drug habits and helped them find jobs in the area. Even the older, most wealthy members embraced these young addicts and helped them stay clean and out of trouble.

One of the young girls, an addict and a lesbian, was taken to Teen Challenge, the same ministry I started out with, and her life was completely turned around. Today she's back in Milwaukee and married to a youth pastor in the area.

Through this process the church began to change. The people gained a new sense of renewal in their faith and their purpose in the community. They saw the impact they could have if they just opened up their homes and hearts. They'd witnessed firsthand what the Holy Spirit could do in the lives of people steeped in sin, and it created within them a taste for evangelism that seemed insatiable. Through their ministry to this small group of wayward kids, they rediscovered their own faith and remembered their first love.

I knew God had orchestrated this miraculous event as a way to bring the people of the congregation together and to create in them a vision for our crusade. Many people who might have never considered helping began to sign up to venture into the inner city with us. Though it was a frightening thought for them, they trusted God, took off their suits and ties, and slipped on our TRUCE T-shirts.

The next offer for help with our crusade came from a large Assembly of God church in one of the outlying suburbs of the city. They introduced us to a handful of ex-addicts and former gang members who also volunteered their time. The pastors of these two churches agreed to serve as cochairmen of our outreach crusade in the city.

This was the team God had called together to work with us in our evangelistic efforts: A wealthy, predominantly white Lutheran church, a large Assembly of God fellowship, and a handful of street kids. It was the most diverse group of people we'd ever partnered with.

We couldn't wait to see what God had in store for us.

RIGHT AND AUTHENTIC

There's nothing quite like seeing God's people put aside their pride and personal prejudices and come together in unity to reach the lost. Watching these rich and educated professional people walking alongside former gang members and prostitutes, donning TRUCE T-shirts, and passing out tracts and Bibles to inner-city children was a powerful testimony to God's goodness. We were no longer black or white, Asian or Spanish, rich or poor; we were only a group of Christians helping people in the name of Jesus. There was something very right and authentic about it—something that moved us all deeply.

During one of our first hit-and-run outreaches in one of the most gang-infested sections of the city, we felt God's anointing rain down upon our efforts. We attracted a frightening crowd of angry teens, drug dealers, prostitutes, and gang members, and I worried for the safety of our suburban friends. But God gave us all a spirit of boldness.

Across the street from where we set up, there was a house that held an obvious drug ring. While the Christian rap singers performed for the crowd that had gathered, we noticed a steady stream of cars pull up to the curb and walk up to the front door, usually glaring at us from over their shoulders. A man would answer, and drugs and money would exchange hands. They didn't even try to hide what they were doing.

When the music died down, one of our youth volunteers stepped forward to give his testimony. He was a kid from their city, a former drug dealer who had experienced the saving hand of Jesus. His story was their story.

We could feel God's Spirit moving in the hearts of the people, and when the young man finished sharing, many people came forward to accept Christ. A few of them handed over forty-ounce bottles of liquor to our volunteers and asked for prayer. Others were on their knees, confessing their sins and begging for God's forgiveness as our volunteers embraced them and prayed with them.

Several of our TRUCE workers felt God's leading them to talk to the people across the street who had been dealing drugs. A few people had come out of the house and were watching us from the front porch. The front of the house had recently been sprayed with bullets in a drive-by shooting by rival gang members. As our volunteers started across, they were surprised that the people didn't run for cover. Our workers told them about Jesus, and one of the men accepted Christ. Right on his doorstep, a prominent doctor from the Lutheran church hugged him and prayed with him.

God was clearly smiling on our efforts, sending his Spirit to confirm that he was indeed pleased with our compassion for the lost and our willingness to work together as one body for one divine and holy purpose.

That same sense of unity and oneness in the Spirit stayed with us throughout the weeks and months to come as we continued reaching out and ministering in Jesus' name. Everywhere we went we could feel God's hand leading and guiding, taking us right to the curbs and doorsteps where we were needed most.

GANG AGAINST GANG

One day we heard of an escalating threat between two rival girl gangs, so we set out to find them. For some reason, girl gangs are often the most violent and dangerous to deal with. I'm not sure I understand why they're so dangerous—perhaps they feel they have more to prove—but most people in the streets will attest to this fact.

We found one of the gangs on a corner and began telling them about Jesus. Several got angry and left, but a few held back to talk to us. Over the next hour we were able to lead many of these women to Christ. The volunteers embraced them, prayed with them, then promised to get them help. They followed through on that promise over the months to come, and soon most of these girls were off the streets and working in jobs around the city.

During another street outreach concert we learned of a recent drive-by shooting that had taken the life of a young gang member and his girlfriend. We found out where the girl's parents lived, and Patrick and Alicia decided to make a visit to share our condolences over their loss. They didn't see it as an outreach strategy, just a way to show people that we cared. We sensed that the Holy Spirit was guiding us to them, so Patrick and Alicia took a handful of people and went to visit them in their home.

The two had been killed in front of the girl's house, and a shrine in their memory had been created at the base of a large tree in front of the home. It was surrounded by candles and filled with photos and notes and flowers and stuffed animals placed there by friends and family members. Patrick and Alicia spent time consoling and praying with these poor people. Before the evening ended, they led the entire family to Jesus.

FURTHER RESULTS

These are just a few of the many powerful stories of salvation that came out of our ministry to this hardened city. It would be impossible to chronicle the full impact of our outreach campaign on the people of this community. And it was often hard to tell which group was being ministered to the most—the people of the inner city or the unlikely team of volunteers that God had orchestrated to help us. As usual, God's blessing was a bilateral one.

Over the coming weeks, more and more people were coming to Christ each day, and word of this began to spread like fire throughout the city's Christian community. Each time we went to the streets we had new faces among us. People were catching the vision. We had people from almost every imaginable denomination and label helping us—Southern Baptists, Methodists, Presbyterians, Pentecostals, Church of God, Charismatic, independent, nondenominational—you name it. By the end of the crusade, we had representatives from more than thirty local congregations working alongside us, including a born-again, Spirit-filled Catholic nun! She was a spitfire of a woman who loved talking about Jesus.

Local high schools were feeling the impact we were making on the kids of the city, and began calling us to see what they could do to help. Many invited me to speak in their assemblies, and almost every morning I went to a different school to share my faith and testimony in their assemblies. I spoke at some of the most violent and gang-infested high schools in the area, yet they never showed any disrespect. Each time I spoke, the kids listened intently and flooded to the front afterward to talk to me.

After six months of ministry to the inner city, it was finally time for our nine-day presentation of the *Run Baby Run* stage production at a college auditorium. Each night the auditorium was packed long before showtime.

We were witnessing firsthand what God is willing to do when the body of Christ comes together as one to reach people with the gospel. When we put away our personal agendas and theological differences and focus instead on a greater good—the saving of human souls—the Holy Spirit comes alive with power in our midst.

When the Christians in Milwaukee decided to come together in unity, to forget their fear and apathy toward the inner city, and to instead follow the leading of the Holy Spirit, it made an impact on their city that's still being felt today. Literally thousands were brought to Christ because of their faithfulness. It was a beautiful thing to witness.

A MAYOR'S GRATITUDE

At the end of our six-month love affair with Milwaukee, I got a call from the mayor. He'd been watching and hearing about the impact we were making on his city and wanted to meet with me.

From the moment I walked into his plush office, I could sense his skepticism. He was polite but reserved. He settled into his oversized leather chair and invited me to take a seat across from him. After a few minutes of polite conversation, he said, "I've heard a lot about your work in the inner city, and I wanted to thank you personally. I'm excited to see some of the changes you've made."

I smiled and nodded as he took a big sip of coffee.

"Thank you for your interest," I told him, "but it's not really me who has made a difference. It is Jesus."

He leaned back and folded his arms across his chest. "I'm sure it is," he said, somewhat condescending. "But still I'd like to thank you."

He took a long pause, then leaned forward, folding his arms across the top of his large cherry desk. "Tell me something," he continued. "Do you honestly believe that you can just lay hands on a person, casting out some kind of demon or something, and that he'll be changed forever?"

I sat forward in my chair and looked him in the eye. "I believe that Jesus can come in and change any person, no matter how hard or angry he or she is. There are none so lost or desperate or violent that God can't change their hearts. I know because that's what he did for me."

I knew I had his attention, so I began to share my testimony. I told him about my days in Puerto Rico as a child, how my parents were immersed in the occult, how they sent me to live in New York because they could no longer control me. I told him of my days as the leader of the Mau Maus, and of the hate and violence I had seen and inflicted. I told him of my liberation from hell at the feet of Jesus.

By the time I finished he was leaning forward in his chair with one knee on the floor and his mouth wide open. He told me he'd never heard a story so brutal.

"I know you hate gangs and gang members," I told him. "You'd like to just lock them all away so you won't have to deal with them anymore. I don't blame you, because I know what they do to your city. But let me tell you what I've seen in your streets. A lot of these kids don't want to be there. They're in gangs and doing drugs because they don't see any way out. They're lost, and they don't think anyone cares about them. Those are the kids you need to be trying to reach. They want to change and they deserve a chance.

"I'm aware that there are some kids who aren't willing to change, and they need to be held accountable. They need to be locked up and made to pay for their actions. I'm not asking you to be soft on crime. I'm asking you to make an effort to help the ones who are trying to get out, trying to turn their lives around. Otherwise, you'll never be able to heal this city and the animosity that exists here."

I sensed his heart softening as he listened and received my words of advice.

"Sometimes I try to imagine what would have happened to me if I hadn't been given a second chance," I told him. "I praise God that he loved me enough to do that."

Over the next few hours we continued to discuss the problems in his city, and I was able to share with him many of my ideas about helping kids out of the lifestyle of gangs and drugs and crime. He and I shared a common interest—healing the pain of his city's urban area. And it led him to reevaluate many of his preconceived ideas about the inner city.

Since that meeting, many changes have taken shape within the city of Milwaukee. The mayor immediately put together a task force to study the problem and invited teams from other large cities to help advise them on the different programs and approaches that are working elsewhere. He encouraged local foundations to help fund faith-based organizations that were trying to reach out to the inner city. Slowly, changes began to take shape. Recently the city donated a seven-building, six-million-dollar hospital to the local Assembly of God churches to be used for a medical ministry to inner-city people.

Today the city of Milwaukee has come a long way toward turning their problems around. Though there's a long way to go, Milwaukee is now seen as a city in transition, a city of compassion for the poor and helpless. Other cities are now looking to it for advice on how to deal with gang violence and crime.

We could easily try to give man the credit for these changes, but it's easy to see that God is the one who put this city on the path to healing. And it all started when a handful of mismatched Christians came together under the direction of the Holy Spirit to reach kids with the gospel.

At no time is the Holy Spirit's power manifested more mightily in the hearts and lives of believers than when we're one in heart and purpose.

CHAPTER TWENTY-ONE

A vision
of love and unity

In this final chapter, let me take you once more to something that God did in Milwaukee. Several years ago I was invited to speak at a large high school in Milwaukee's inner city. Crime and gang activity had run out of control in and around the school grounds, forcing the school board to create a task force to study the problem. The committee saw no way of stopping the violence and fighting among the students and recommended that the city close the school. In a last-ditch effort they brought me in to talk to the kids, hoping my testimony and message would bring a measure of peace to the situation.

I didn't know it at the time, but in the audience that day, sitting on opposite sides of the auditorium, were two rival gang leaders—one named Luis, the other Ricky. The two had spent much of their lives as sworn enemies. Though they were young, their years had been filled with violence and rage against each other, fighting at every opportunity, often for no discernible reason. These were turf wars, an excuse to kill and maim and vent.

Both Luis and Ricky went home that day unrepentant, but a seed had been planted through my testimony.

"I Hated You So Much"

As the months went by, the violence between the two gangs only escalated. Gang members were constantly in trouble, in and out of jail, and watched carefully by the police. Many feared that their anger would some day culminate into an explosion of violence, so careful people kept their distance.

One day Luis, who was Puerto Rican, was caught stealing and was forced to serve a four-month sentence in the local jail. A prison missionary gave him a copy of my book *Run Baby Run,* and he read it cover to cover. It affected him deeply. He later said it read like a documentary of his own life. He prayed that God would help him turn his life around, and when he got out of jail he began attending a local church, determined to make an effort. A few weeks later Luis went forward during an altar call and gave his life to Christ.

Some time later, Ricky (who was still terrorizing the neighborhood) was invited by an inner-city evangelist to hear the legendary football player Reggie White speak at a local church. He went only to hear some good football stories, but he found himself convicted by Reggie's testimony. He went forward afterward to meet and talk with his idol, though he wasn't yet ready to make a commitment. Reggie stayed in touch with Ricky, inviting him to Bible studies and other events, and four months later Ricky came to Christ.

Several months afterward, through a unique series of circumstances, these two former gang leaders and rivals found themselves at a Bible study in the home of one of my ministry workers. It was the first time they'd seen each other since their days on the streets.

For several minutes neither knew what to say. There was a noticeable tension in the air. Suddenly Luis pointed to a large scar on his cheek. "Remember this? You did this when you smashed my face with a phone."

The two laughed nervously. Then Ricky said half-jokingly, "Yeah, I do. But do you remember what you did to my friend? You hit him over the head with a hammer!"

Again the two snickered in amusement.

"Remember that day you were standing by the curb, and someone in a car came by and started shooting at you?" Ricky asked.

Luis thought for a moment. "Yeah, I remember that. I almost got killed."

"Well, that was me."

For a moment they were silent, then Luis said, "Do you remember the time you were riding your motorcycle down the street and a bullet from a .357 went right by your head?"

"Yeah, I do!" said Ricky. "I saw someone running, but I couldn't see their face."

"That was me," Luis admitted.

For the next half-hour the boys reminisced about their days as enemies before finding Christ. They talked of the hate and contempt they once felt, confessing their feelings of anger and resentment toward each other.

At one point Luis turned to Ricky with tears streaming down the sides of his face. "I hated you so much I used to lie awake at night wondering how to kill you. I wanted to cut you into little pieces and scatter your body all over the street for people to see. Now here we are together, and I don't hate you any more. Jesus has taken away the hate. Now you're my brother!"

Before long they were buried in each other's arms, crying and asking for forgiveness. My ministry worker walked over and embraced the two as they wept. He explained that, as he held them to his chest, he could feel God's Spirit come in and cleanse them, replacing their hate with love and humility toward each other. His shirt was drenched with their tears. Once they were able to humble themselves and confess their feelings of resentment and anger, God was able to wrap his arms around them and bring emotional healing to their hearts and souls.

Several weeks later Luis and Ricky were working side-by-side, preaching about Jesus in the streets of the inner city. Kids in the neighborhood couldn't believe their eyes. Here were two former enemies, once filled with hate and rage, now working together to bring a message of love to the streets they once terrorized.

"BEAST" IS KILLED

Luis and Ricky ran across another former gang member—a boy they called "Beast"—and Ricky stayed back to witness to him. "You need Jesus, Beast," he told him. "He can change your life forever."

After a few minutes, Beast looked at Ricky and asked, "How old were you when you found Jesus?"

"Twenty-six," he answered.

"Well, I'm only twenty-three," Beast snickered, "so I guess I've got three more years!"

Ricky continued to witness to him, but his words fell on deaf ears. Eventually Beast tired of the conversation and walked away.

The next morning, Beast was shot and killed by a policeman on the steps of a church building. His time had run out.

Almost immediately the killing of Beast sent the inner city into an uproar. Nearby witnesses claimed that the shooting was unnecessary and intentional—an outright racial murder—and tempers quickly flared within area gangs and the community. Inner-city activists began crying for justice and revenge. They were demanding that someone pay for the killing.

Area churches and civic leaders worried about the escalating tempers within the neighborhood, and immediately they began planning a March Against Violence followed by a community meeting in the basement of a nearby high school. It was to be held a week after Beast's funeral.

The day of the meeting, tempers were still running at fever pitch. Hundreds of gang members—each flaunting their gang colors—joined hostile activists and parents in the high school basement to demonstrate their anger. Folding chairs were packed tightly into the large, dimly lit hall. Smoke filled the room in spite of the school's restriction on cigarettes. Undercover police kept vigil along the entrance and corridors of the building. Many were worried that a riot might break out in the halls of the building.

A MOB IS QUIETED

In the middle of all this anger, sitting on the front row of the meeting hall, were Luis and Ricky. They were asked to speak to the crowd.

The meeting was called to order, and the noise subsided slightly as Luis made the frightening walk up to the front of the restive crowd.

"Most of you know who I am," he began. "I used to be a gang member, but now I preach about Jesus. I used to hate every one of you, but now I'm filled with the love and compassion of Jesus. He has taken away the pain and replaced it with love."

The mob was visibly angry and impatient. They were more interested in revenge than compassion. Some heckled Luis. Still, he continued to speak. He called for mercy and calmness among the crowd, pleading with them to put away their anger and instead look to Jesus for the answers they needed. In frustration, he began to tell them about my book—my testimony—and the healing that Jesus brought into my life once I allowed him to heal my rage and replace it with love.

He sat down, and Ricky took his place at the podium.

"I talked to Beast the night before he was killed," Ricky began.

The crowd grew deathly quiet.

"Now Beast is dead. And I know that if he could come back, he would say to you, 'Find Jesus, because he's real.'"

Ricky paused to let his words sink in. As he continued sharing Christ with the crowd a noticeable change started to take shape. The anger began to subside. Tears began to fall. The peace of God began to settle on the room as Ricky continued calling for love and forgiveness instead of vengeance.

By the end of the meeting the entire tone of the crowd had changed. All over the room people were weeping in shame and repentance. Gang members walked to the front and threw down their gang colors beside the podium. God's Spirit fell on the room, bringing a wave of conviction and calming the hearts of this angry crowd.

The presence of these two former gang leaders who were once bitter enemies but who now joined hands for the cause of peace had touched the crowd deeply—not as a mob but as individual people looking for a better way to vent their rage. In the same city streets where these two young men had once fought bitterly for control, they now stood united, with a single purpose in mind—to help bring the peace of Christ to his people. And because of their oneness in faith and vision, what had begun as a show of hate had suddenly turned into an evening of spiritual reflection and revival.

WHAT JESUS PRAYED FOR

I often wonder what could be accomplished if we did the same thing. What if the body of Christ as a whole could come together in unity, put away our differences of opinions and our social and doctrinal disputes, and focus on one specific goal—to reach the lost? What if we called on the Holy Spirit to heal the wounds and bring forgiveness to our hearts and souls—forgetting the past and concentrating instead on the future? What kind of spiritual revival would the world experience when they saw us standing together before them in a united front?

That's the kind of love and unity that Jesus, our big Brother and Savior, prayed for just before going to the cross:

> I pray also for those who will believe in me through their message, that all of them may be one, Father, just as you are in me and I am in you. May they also be in us so that the world may believe that you have sent me. I have given them the glory that you gave me, that they may be one as we are one: I in them and you in me. May they be brought to

complete unity to let the world know that you sent me and have loved them even as you have loved me. (John 17:20-23)

Jesus prayed for unity among his followers because he knew that without it we would be helpless in the midst of an angry and hostile world. It's only through a unified spirit, through standing together as one against the attacks of the Evil One, that we're able to effectively bring God's message of love and hope to a world steeped in sin. How can we offer peace and love to a chaotic culture if we don't have it within our own ranks?

Paul taught this same kind of unity in purpose:

Make every effort to keep the unity of the Spirit through the bond of peace. There is one body and one Spirit—just as you were called to one hope when you were called—one Lord, one faith, one baptism; one God and Father of all, who is over all and through all and in all. (Ephesians 4:3-6)

I long to see the day when Christians everywhere rise up in unity to once and for all ask every person on this planet to bow their knees before our merciful Savior. That would be a day humankind would never forget—the day Jesus' followers came together with one heart, one mind, one Spirit, and one purpose: to release one holy fire upon the world!

IF YOU WONDER

If you're a believer who still wonders about God's vision and purpose for your life, someone who hasn't found an all-consuming passion in your Christian walk, I plead with you to do so. Go to the Lord and ask for clear direction and guidance, for a vision, for your divine and specific role in his greater plan. Beg him to use you, to mold and mentor you, to fill you, and to empty you out in his service.

Don't take God's wonderful grace for granted. Don't keep it to yourself. Share his love and forgiveness with the world around you, with the people who need Jesus. Let Jesus touch your eyes again, so that you can see people the way that he sees them. Take the poor and thirsty by the hand and lead them to drink at the well of God's goodness. Life is much too short to be spent simply gratifying our own needs and desires. Leave a legacy that matters.

afterword

In his letter to the Galatians, the apostle Paul wrote, "If we live in the Spirit, let us also walk in the Spirit" (Galatians 5:25, KJV). Throughout Scripture it is clear that God's purpose for every one of his children is that we surrender to the reign and rulership of the Holy Spirit. In fact, the Spirit's primary purpose for living within us is to direct and guide us in all that we do.

The Holy Spirit provides absolute and detailed instructions to those who walk in him. When we walk in the Spirit, we don't walk in confusion or doubt. His direction is clear and distinct. The early disciples of Christ understood this truth, and they allowed the Spirit to direct them in every decision, every move, every action. The Spirit talked to them and guided them in their every waking hour. No decisions were made without first consulting him. The church's motto throughout the New Testament was, "He who has ears to hear, let him hear what the Spirit has to say."

You and I have that same opportunity today. The same Spirit that guided the early believers in their walk with the Lord is living within you and me, beckoning us daily to listen, to submit, to heed his will and direction. He promises power and effectiveness beyond our wildest dreams. The only remaining question is, *Will we allow him to reign?*

One Holy Fire is Nicky Cruz's clarion call for all believers to not only understand this amazing truth, but to finally embrace it. More than any person I know, Nicky Cruz is a living testament to God's unmistakable power and mercy. He stands today as a monument to the Holy Spirit's ability to completely change and redirect a person's life and heart.

The message of this book is as simple as it is critical: *The Holy Spirit can change your life and ignite your soul!* Nicky's life and ministry are living proof of that truth. And the wisdom God has imparted into and through him is nothing short of miraculous.

Whatever you do, don't come away from this reading without embracing and heeding this important and powerful message. Let God use this book to change your life and ignite your soul!

PASTOR DAVID WILKERSON
TIMES SQUARE CHURCH

acknowledgments

I'd like to give heartfelt thanks to the following people for their help and support.

To Patrick and Alicia Dow, for their tireless dedication to the ministry, and their help with this project. Their many stories and insights were invaluable.

To Rob Goraieb, my son-in-law, for his diligent research and work during the beginning stages of this project, and for encouraging me to get these thoughts into a book.

To Karen Robinson, who worked closely with Frank and me in all the little details, and to all of my faithful staff. Thanks, Judy, for helping me get to where I need to go.

To Thomas Womack, at WaterBrook Press—the one editor who I knew could give life to this book and do justice to the material.

To Frank Martin, my friend and cowriter. And to his beautiful and insightful wife, Ruthie, for sharing her husband's time and energy with me during this long and arduous process.

To Vaso and Trevor, for their constant inspiration, and their skills in handling and negotiating this book project.

And finally, thanks to my beautiful wife, Gloria, for her continued love and inspiration in all I do.

To contact the author:

Nicky Cruz Outreach
P.O. Box 25070
Colorado Springs, Colorado 80936

www.nickycruz.org